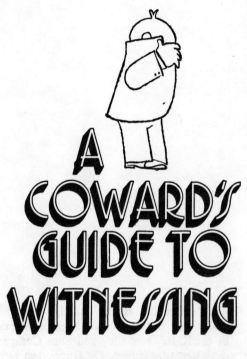

A COWARD'S GUIDE TO WITNESSING

KEN ANDERSON

CREATION HOUSE
Carol Stream, Illinois 60187

© 1972 by Creation House.
Printed in the United States of America
by the R. R. Donnelley and Sons Company
Published by Creation House, 499 Gundersen Drive
Carol Stream, Illinois 60187

First printing (April 1972)--5,000
Second printing (July 1972)--5,000
Third printing (December 1972)--5,000
Fourth printing (November 1973)--5,000

International Standard Book Number 0-88419-023-4
Library of Congress Catalog Card Number 75-189627

To

Ken, Jr.

CONTENTS

1.
Unaccustomed Though I Am . . .

In spite of cowardice, perhaps because of it, a Christian can be assured of giving effective witness.

Days often pass without my having an opportunity to share my faith and, in such Sahara experiences, the judicial leer of guilt all but impells me to take to the streets in bold conquest of the lost world around me.

But I don't.

I can't.

Perhaps you, too, are the kind for whom witnessing comes hard. You can talk about anything from the weather to politics but your tongue goes limp at the thought of relating Christ to someone.

If so, take heart.

Because, however steeped you may be in cowardice, you can learn to so place yourself in God's control that witness will happen again and again in your experience.

Such as, for example, a telephone call I got recently from one of the prominent businessmen in our town.

"Ken," he said, "I'd sure like to talk to you sometime — about your religion."

My heart skipped a beat, in both fear and anticipation.

Because my schedule tends to be perpetually harried so that there is rarely a convenient time, I have learned to say in such situations, "I could see you now."

He came to my office.

"You seem to have been very successful with your family," he began. "What's the secret?"

"There isn't any, Joe," I replied. "In fact, I'm something short, in many ways, of being an exemplary father. I always have deadlines staring at me. I'm gone from my family months at a time, so I can't give them the attention they need. But my wife and I have tried to introduce our children to a living faith."

"How do you do that?"

"Well, first of all, making sure of such a faith yourself. Then living that faith in the presence of your kids."

"My wife and I have tried to do that. We are both members of the church. There isn't anyone more active and dependable or who attends more faithfully than we do."

Tactic here for a lot of Christians would have been to give him a down-with-your-church routine. His church believes Christ automatically assures salvation for every man, that the church's job is to "evangelize" the structures of society, not lost individuals.

"Somehow," he continued, "we can't get the children interested in church. I think it's the fault of the schools, the whole society."

I talked about personal faith, about the antifaith erosions modern thought furrows into the minds of thinking young people. We discussed Toynbee's thesis that every civilization, even in its most golden era, has been destined for decay. I read him excerpts from Francis Schaeffer's *Escape from Reason* and C. S. Lewis' *Screwtape Letters*.

And, of course, we looked penetratingly into the Scriptures.

I knew his church tends to humanize the Word of God, but I made no apology for my full confidence in the Bible, its assessment of man's lostness, the power of the gospel to bring redemption.

"Do you really believe there is a personal devil?" he asked. "How can you be sure the Bible is God's Word? I can't even be sure there's a God. I take it you're talking about conversion. My wife and I have noticed that people who really go

10

big on conversion theology are often the biggest hypocrites."

The questions flew at me like missiles as I shared my faith and the imperative of personal salvation.

After that initial encounter in the office, we moved to several sessions in a small writing shack I have behind our house. I seemed to be making little headway but he kept coming back for more.

One night, after we had talked for several hours, I bluntly said, "Joe, what you need is to admit you are a sinner, that Christ is your only hope, and then open your life to Him."

Hunger came to his eyes, anticipation to my heart.

"I wish I could really believe that," he said.

"Take God at His word, Joe. The Bible tells us that *faith cometh by hearing, and hearing by the word of God.* [1]

He came so close that night!

"You've given me a lot to think about," he said as he left.

But he didn't return, and though we had cordial encounters around town now and then, he evaded my witness.

Each spring our company, which produces audiovisuals geared primarily for use by evangelical churches, sponsors a goodwill dinner for business and professional leaders in town. We show examples of our work, often invite a layman to share his faith—particularly someone associated with a project of ours.

One year, for example, we had Stanley Tam prior to production on the film *God Owns My Business*, based on Stan's effective testimony and witness. Recently we had Redd Harper, during production planning on the film we did with him.

Joe has never missed one of the dinners. At the conclusion of the night with Redd Harper, Joe came to me and exclaimed, "That was tremendous! Ken, it's really wonderful that you people have these dinners and bring in exciting people like Mr. Harper!"

I felt sure Joe would call me the next day.

He didn't.

But only a couple of weeks later, a friend of mine telephoned to tell me he had been talking with Joe and, at the conclusion of the conversation, Joe had opened his heart to Christ.

I was thrilled, of course, but a small edge of envy came also into my thoughts. Why hadn't I been privileged to bring Joe to his time of decision? Was something lacking in my witness? To my mind came the apostle Paul's words, "*I planted, Apollos watered; but God was causing the growth.*" 2

Annually, my wife and I have our physicals at the Mayo Clinic. My consulting physician for the past six years has been a younger member of the staff. Interested in the work we do, he faithfully checks me for any endemics picked up as a result of my numerous and varied overseas assignments.

He works quickly but thoroughly. We usually spend fifteen minutes together.

From the first time we met, I wanted to relate my faith to him. But these men operate on a strategic schedule and, with my inborn reluctance, I could hardly bring myself to say, "Doc, I know you're busy, but...."

Then this past year, as I waited in the outer area for my appointment, a strong persuasion came over me.

I was to talk to this doctor about my faith in Jesus Christ.

The thought both frightened and stimulated me!

Perenially the coward, I silently cried out, *Lord, how can I do it? This is the Mayo Clinic. Every minute of a doctor's time is like gold.*

So slow I am to learn the ways of the Holy Spirit!

"What were you doing this past year, Mr. Anderson?" the doctor asked when the examination began.

I had just returned from an extended assignment in Vietnam. This caught his fancy and, when he completed the initial examination and would normally have sent me on to my three-day schedule of tests, he sat on the edge of his desk and asked, "What's going to happen in the world?"

I knew the Holy Spirit had opened the door!

Like a small boy in Sunday school, he listened as I gave him my witness.

Several times I interrupted myself, saying, "Look, Doc, you've got a heavy schedule," and each time he gestured for me to continue.

He gave me twenty minutes!

Then, glancing at his watch, he asked, "Do you think the world is going to make it, Mr. Anderson?"

"Frankly, I get a little pessimistic at times," I replied.

"So do I."

I spoke of the ecological panic beginning to stalk the globe, the rape of nature by men motivated by materialism, the stark economic pressures on one nation inclined to clean up its air and water while competing nations produced goods with no more than casual thought to pollution.

"But the crucial issue isn't whether or not the world is going to make it," I said. "Am I going to make it? Are you going to make it?"

His eyes were intent upon me.

"The only way we can make it," I continued, "is through a redeeming relationship with God in Jesus Christ."

Silence fell upon the office for a moment. I had poise and courage beyond myself. And I knew, absolutely without doubt, that my encounter with this doctor was the doing of the Holy Spirit, I being only the tool in His hands.

He glanced at his watch again, reluctance coming to his manner.

"I really appreciate talking to you," he said. Then he sent me on to my schedule of tests.

It's a wonderful arrangement, witnessing under the guidance of the Holy Spirit. I must not chafe at the infrequency of occasions when the witness involves an opportunity for me to participate in actual harvest. I am a tool, fashioned by my Lord for His purposes here upon earth. It is for Him to determine how the tool will be employed.

But the Bible does tell us, *"He that goeth forth weeping,*

bearing precious seed, shall doubtless come again with rejoicing, bringing his sheaves with him." [3] And I thank God for those times when, even in my witness, I the coward have participated in the culmination of harvest.

Recently for example, a salesman of audiovisual products came to my office. I was very busy, he didn't have a prior appointment, and I didn't want to see him.

"Send him into the conference room," I told my secretary. That way I could excuse myself whenever I wished.

He was an obviously troubled man and, after a brief discourse on his line of goods, I found myself brought naturally into a sharing of my faith.

"I haven't a clue what you're talking about," he said as his eyes indicated how desperately he wanted to know.

I prayed for guidance. We talked for over an hour, and I endeavored several times to bend the conversation, to ask him to make a decision, but I felt restrained.

"I have another appointment," he said at last, and my spirits fell, "but I've got to talk to you some more. Will you be home tonight?"

Nights are given to free-lance writing out in the shack, and I was at that time on a tight deadline.

Would you believe I almost put him off? But the Holy Spirit firmly reprimanded me.

"Sure," I said, "I've got a place behind the house where we can talk alone. How about eight o'clock?"

He arrived on the minute, interrupting me in the middle of a flowing paragraph.

"I'm going to tell you something I've never told another human being," he began. "I've got a wonderful wife and family. But out calling a couple of years ago, I met the wife of one of the suppliers we serve. He was gone. It was a rainy day. She was alone in the store. She's a fine woman, and I've always considered myself a decent sort, but we got involved. It's turned into a nasty case of secret adultery."

I could write chapters on what he told me. Let it suffice

14

to say the Holy Spirit freshened my mind with concepts beyond myself as—in a somewhat nonecclesiastical manner but, I am convinced, thoroughly scriptural approach—the Holy Spirit helped me show this man how Christ could deliver him from the grime and guilt in his life.

He laughed and wept simultaneously as victory came to his tormented body that night.

About midnight he said, "Would you be willing to talk to this woman?"

I recoiled at first. Clandestine women don't sit too well with my rather wholesome agrarian background.

But I managed to say, "I would see her with my wife present."

He hesitated. "I'm not sure she would want to meet your wife," he said.

"She's not from this town?" I asked in disbelief.

"She lives a little over a hundred miles from here. I'll give her a call first thing in the morning. I know she wants to get this mess straightened out the same as I did."

The next morning he called.

"She's willing to come see you," he said. "Her husband's going to be gone to a convention, and she could be there by 8:00 o'clock Wednesday morning."

My wife didn't like the idea any more than I had initially.

"I'd want you to meet her at the door," I said.

The forthcoming visit occupied much of our thoughts and prayers and, in the evening, my wife told me, "I've decided that, when I meet her at the door, I can tell her she has a lot of courage. I can do that honestly."

Morning came.

Eight o'clock.

We waited.

At about ten minutes after eight, a car drove into the yard, a woman we had not seen before got out and came toward the door.

My wife met her.

15

"God bless you!" I heard my wife exclaim. "You've got lots of courage!"

Then the woman stepped inside, and she and my wife literally melted into each other's arms.

She was a lovely person, as unlikely a candidate for marital chicanery as one could imagine.

"I just don't know how it ever happened," she said over and over, "because I have such a wonderful husband, and I love him so much, but I'm just like someone in chains."

"Do you want to be free from those chains?" I asked.

"With all my heart!"

Then, with all my heart, I assured her, "I can tell you that Jesus Christ can set you free. That's what His gospel is all about — liberating people from the power of sin."

Liberation came to this dear soul that morning. As my wife and I knelt, one on either side of the chair where she sat, each of us sensed the electrifying move of the Holy Spirit as transformation enveloped that woman's body.

The Holy Spirit *does* lead and empower.

God *will* use us.

We are inept within ourselves, yet as strategic as the wire which conveys electrical current.

I cannot explain the fact of sin, the awesome statistic whereby we know world overpopulation involves the birth of far more people than we can ever hope to reach for Christ at our present rate of evangelistic endeavor.

But I do know the gospel is, most assuredly, *"the power of God for salvation to every one who believes."* [4]

We recently had some of the "Jesus People" as guests in our home, sat spellbound as they related their exploration into the sinister world of drug dimensions, heard them tell how Christ had come to make the difference.

"We know the gospel is real," one of them said, "because we weren't only spiritually lost, we were dying physically. The Lord Jesus not only saved our souls, but He transformed our bodies."

16

"My mind was all broken up in little fragments from four years on acid," another said, "but when I came to Jesus, He put my mind all back together again."

Broken homes, broken lives, broken minds—all can experience the touch of Christ and transformation.

And if we will obey God, all us who know Him, those who need this message will hear it.

You may be familiar with the frightening mathematics by which one can tabulate that, were you the only believer in the world and led one person to Christ this year, and then you and that person each led another to Christ the following year—in less than thirty-five years, everyone in the world would be converted.

Obedience.

That's the key.

And however deep the trauma of cowardice, we can experience obedience, for God never asks us to obey an order for which He does not also provide courage and strength.

If you could know me and take a close look at the basic ineptitude I have for witnessing, you'd understand why that simple concept means so much to me.

And, I would hope and pray, perhaps you'd glean some guidance and courage for your own life.

Color me yellow...

2.
Join the Club

It's not easy to admit lack of courage, but it's the place to start if you want to gain boldness in your witness.

No matter how you phrase it, however polite or sympathetic you may be, by basic generics my status as a witness of the Christian faith stands clearly defined.

I'm a coward.

Oh, I like the ego-pampering some of my friends give me. As a producer of church-related motion pictures, my activity involves global travel and consequent experiences which, given the hyperbolic touch, could make for rather flamboyant parlor conversation.

In 1948, for example, Bob Pierce invited me to trek with him extensively across the mainland of China, through hazardous areas where one sometimes found himself hard put to determine whose allegiance belonged to Mao Tse-tung and whose to Chiang Kai-shek.

During the Communist bid for Malaya, I traveled north out of Singapore to a filming assignment in an area not yet cleared of guerilla bands. On the rubber plantation where we worked, travel had to be done by armored car, and government soldiers gunned down an infiltrator outside the window of one of our location areas.

While Vietnam made worldwide headlines, my work took me on a number of projects in that tormented area, including a sequence in Hue during Tet holidays. It was commonplace to the missionaries where we stayed, but one night in DaNang a rocket attack punctuated our schedule. One afternoon,

19

working among tribesmen outside Dalat, our photographer had a hunch, set the zoom lens on telephoto, panned out across the hills and declared he caught sight of a VC watching our activities.

The Indo-China experience also included a helicopter combat mission with U.S. Army Rangers. Add to these experiences an assignment fifteen miles from rebel-held territory in Congo, three weeks on a documentary in beleaguered Biafra, a mob of surly villagers in India, Masai warriors in Kenya threatening to smash our equipment—not to mention being charged by a wild elephant, jaunting miles through primitive cobra country, and going for nightly swims in a small lake we subsequently discovered to be infested with crocodiles.

Oh, yes, I'm also unafraid of thunder and lightning!

But when it comes to talking to someone about his need for personal salvation, a broad, luminous yellow streak runs from the nape of my neck all the way down to the base of my spine.

I want to give effective witness of my faith—it is a constant compulsion in my life, but cowardice has given me an uncanny knack at coming up with excuses for not articulating my faith to others.

Very spiritual excuses, I should add. Often quite acceptable to the evangelical establishment.

Christians excel at the art of scoring vicarious touchdowns while basking in the stands under the glow of an October sun. We hire preachers, write checks to biblical causes, faithfully attend church, sing in choirs, serve on committees, avow our silent but sure allegiance to the faith once delivered. Anything to keep from openly and personally and individually communicating our belief in Jesus Christ to those looking for the kind of answers found only in faith.

We even get into the battle itself, but preferably in a we-they relationship and rarely or never in an I-you relationship.

Take me, for example.

Early in my Christian life, my wife challenged me to try free-lance writing. It was a lark at first. I took a fling at secular markets, explored the religious press, and in barely more than two years found myself full time at the typewriter.

To the novice—or at least to my kind of novice—writing tends to be a glamorous venture, complete with muses, delusions of grandeur, and fans.

In my case, I bypassed magazine articles and short stories and sneaked up into the world of churchly culture by writing a novel. And, very nearly to my downfall, getting it published.

Visions of greatness now became figments of reality as, barely into my twenties, I looked forward to a life of fame and affluence. Then came the China experience with Bob Pierce and my first front-on confrontation with the fact of how much materialism motivated my life.

The world never looked the same to me again. Nor did a sheet of paper in a typewriter. I still wrote for a living, but now my objective was to use the typewriter to introduce Christ and the Christian way of life to those who read my copy. Some modestly impressive paragraphs could be written about the people whose lives God touched as a result of reading words which came from my proverbial pen.

Free-lance writing led to motion pictures when C. O. Baptista, pioneer producer of films for evangelical churches, asked me to do a script, subsequently suggested I direct the film and, as a consequence, launched me upon a career in which the camera supplanted what, after twenty years, continues to be my first love, the typewriter.

But though the film business thrives on tension, it quickly made the leisured days of full-time free-lancing a thing of the past, for meeting and hearing of so many people whom the Holy Spirit had touched through one of our films drove me incessantly onward.

Yet, all the while, a shadow of guilt lay across my heart.

People came to Christ as a result of things I had written. Films influenced the hearts of others. "Your ministry touches the lives of many people," my friends said.

Beautiful!

But when it came to personal witness, silence.

As I say, however, I had good excuses. For instance, it deeply distresses me to transgress the rights, particularly the privacy, of others. A noble virtue, in its right perspective. On the other hand, my conscience reminded me, one could hardly be called uncouth for awakening a slumbering neighbor because his roof was on fire.

In a day when the theology of universalism debilitates evangelistic concern among so many believers, I must constantly combat my knack for seeing around a man's lostness and trying to rationalize him into the kingdom.

When, as the result of a tragic farm accident, I stood at the casket of a boyhood friend, agonizing over my failure to make salvation clear to him, I remembered his exemplary ways, the rare occasions when I had casually related Christ to him, and very nearly convinced myself of his salvation— knowing, deep within my conscience, I had disobeyed again and again the promptings of the Holy Spirit.

Pride welled up in my heart when sometimes two and three years in succession, the Internal Revenue Service would question the amount of contributions my wife and I had made to Christian organizations. Faithfulness to the cause surely involves writing checks and dropping paper-printed green into offering baskets.

And I always held in abeyance, for those moments when my conscience punished me most relentlessly, the predominant dodge found in my bag of excuses, namely, the fact that I am, by nature, introverted. A lot of people don't suspect this, including some of my closest friends, because it's a deficiency I've been struggling to correct for several decades.

I can drum up a good bit of self-pity on this score.

My mother, who died on the day of my birth, was of artistic bent. Deeply hurt by the loss, my father did not remarry. He never overtly told me so, but in the retrospect of later years, I feel quite sure he resented me because of my mother's demise. In any case, the two of us never quite hit it off when I was a child and, as a teenager, the gap between us widened.

My father criticized me for the slightest reason. I can never recall the time he put his hand on my shoulder and complimented me. His silence was the only commendation I knew.

The day came when I was sure I hated my father, and not until the declining years of his life could I show him true affection. Only a child who has experienced it understands the depth and the duration of trauma inflicted by parental rejection.

But my father was not the only architect of my frustrations. I received my primary and secondary education at one of those rural consolidated schools which once dotted the Iowa countryside. My cousins, as well as all the young people from the church which I grudgingly attended, went to a larger school in town. This isolated me as a frequent target of ridicule, characteristic to childhood but only understood in adult retrospection.

Athletics made you or broke you those days, and during grade school I tended to be a gawky, uncoordinated farm boy. I was all thumbs and knees, laughably thin, and suffered the ignominy of it all so deeply that I spent hours sharpening my proficiency.

Because our school was small, I made the basketball squad in high school, actually won some citations in league play and tournaments, and as a result silenced most of the tirades which had been coming my way.

But the damage had been done, the scars of insecurity furrowed deep into my frame of reference.

The day I arrived at Wheaton College, I stood on the

sidewalk fringing the campus like a child at a pool, reluctant to dive into cold water.

Dorm mates included a sophisticated musician from Philadelphia, a handsome hockey player from Toronto, a suave business major from Boston. Not a farm boy in the lot.

My roommate not only possessed a valid family coat of arms but could document the fact his forebears came across the Atlantic on the *Mayflower*! Even the subsequent discovery that the *Mayflower* made some forty voyages did not alleviate much of the awe and smallness I felt in his presence.

Some comfort has come to me through the years in the discovery of fellow pilgrims who share my dilemma. My paths frequently cross with an individual who seems abundantly endowed with personal poise and self-confidence. When we get to know each other well enough to stop playing games, however, this person—as you can understand, to my secret delight!—reveals himself as one similarly plagued by insecurity.

We use a number of professional motion-picture actors. A fascinating lot, most of whom appear to be extroverts. Some are. But I remember one talented chap we featured in a film several years ago. Genius radiated from his manner. He was a fine performer, an engaging personality, and during the weeks we worked together we struck up a warm personal friendship.

"Actually, I'm two people," he told me one day. "I get in front of the camera, or I emcee a big promotion, and I come off looking like the guy who could whip the world. I have moments of supreme self-confidence, but more often I'm a dishrag inside. I just don't really believe in myself. I'll be on top for awhile but, with the slightest provocation, or maybe even just something fired out from my subconscious, it's gone."

I lack my actor friend's artistic prowess but I, too, can rise nobly to the occasion under certain circumstances, then cringe in the face of strange or inclement encounters or, like my friend, succumb to something looming up from the past, often unidentified.

Back in high school, our county newspaper launched a subscription drive. I entered and, for the first week, called only on friends and relatives, nearly all of whom subscribed.

So, early in the contest, the newspaper published my name among the front runners. Others eyed me enviously. My ego soared. My anticipation, too, for the top prize was a new automobile, quite an objective during those depression years prior to income taxes as we now know them.

With the depletion of prospects of relatives and friends, however, my zeal waned for an enterprise in which success now depended upon ringing unknown doorbells.

Setting out into strange farming communities, my first stop proved disastrous. The woman of the house not only wasn't interested, she was insolent.

Crestfallen, I headed toward the next farmstead. But the dog came out of the gate, barking and nipping at the car wheels.

So I drove on.

At the next farm I again slowed down. There was no dog. The place appeared friendly. But, devoid of courage, I pressed my foot against the throttle.

Mile after mile I drove, not stopping at so much as one farmhouse until, discouraged and disgusted with myself, I drove home and gave up the contest. Fear of the unknown had once again taken its toll.

This fear stalks me even yet, like a Gargantua. It infuriates me. Why must I be so sure of myself in one circumstance, so cowardly in another? Setting up a filming session in the governor's office becomes routine, while a far less imposing assignment knots my stomach.

My library contains volumes on self-evaluation and improvement. I didn't major in psychology but know many of the phobias by name and have a better-than-average

25

comprehension of what frustrates people and how to talk yourself out of apprehension.

Yet, by any definition you choose to give, you must color me a coward, a trait never more pronounced than when I would articulate my Christian faith in one-to-one relationships.

So it's a lost cause for us timid souls who would do meaningful exploits for our God?

Not necessarily!

For all my weakness—and I sometimes think because of it!—my life is periodically punctuated by witnessing adventures so rewarding as to cause me to be in constant awe of God and His ways with me. Times of deepest discouragement often give rise, pardon the cliche, to mountaintops of victory.

It can be the same for you. Your insecurities may not run as deep as mine—let's hope not—but even if they do, even if they run deeper, take courage.

Personality weaknesses need not necessarily be debits in the life of a Christian. Not at all. On the contrary, weaknesses can be made to work for you instead of against you. It can be a discipline, a catalyst, turning you to dependence upon strength beyond yourself, resources greater by multiples than the human confidence and prowess you envy in others.

But you can't succeed by yourself.

You need help.

God's help!

God *will* help you too. He is committed to do it. First, though, you need to make careful assessment of your motivations.

Be sure, for example, you avoid equating your desires with the preferred will of God. The Adamic strain endows most humans, including the best of Christians, with an uncanny penchant for helping God determine what is best for them.

A meek person, fettered by inadequacy, calls out to God

26

for release and strength and envisions becoming another Billy Graham or Dale Evans.

It could happen.

Cowardly Peter became the eloquent proclaimer of Pentecost.

More likely, though, God will work within your weakness rather than make you emerge from it.

As humans we long to escape. The status quo becomes a mire of frustration and boredom. Like cattle at the fence, our mouths water for the grass beyond reach.

Christians justify their dissatisfactions with what might be called a kind of sacri-altruism. That is, we want our stammering tongues to become eloquent, our stunted personalities to exude magnetism. We want the bloom of miracle to erase the blush of temporal frailty. All within a noble frame of reference calculated to glorify God in the end result, mind you, but underscored by a larger yen for our own convenience and self-centeredness.

In the exuberance of our expectations, as we permit personal desire to affront providential direction, we forget God has told us, *"My grace is sufficient for you, for power is perfected in weakness."* [1]

Your weakness!

Mine!

To be sure, God uses dynamics in human personality, cleverness, talents, but first of all God needs you and me just as we are, just as He fashioned us when we were made for this world.

If, like me, you suffer from cowardice, go to God for prognosis and treatment. Avoid my mistake of listening to others.

"There's a sin in your life, Ken," an older Christian told me during one of the initial years in my Christian walk. "Until you put that sin out of your life, you'll never have freedom in witnessing to others."

Only God knows how long I anguished over that morsel of abortive counseling!

27

Not for a moment ought we to condone sin, for God intends the normal Christian life to be one of victory. But the devil is a master practician. Chief among his ploys is the bleak furrow of guilt. Many a Christian has persecuted himself into ineptitude because of a guilt complex.

I nearly did.

But victory has come to my life, and victory can come to yours.

"Thanks be to God, who always leads us in His triumph in Christ," the Bible reassures us, *"and manifests through us the sweet aroma of the knowledge of Him in every place."* 2

"Always" includes triumph over weakness!

For, if God perfects His strengths in our weakness, then weakness isn't really weakness, it is latent strength, raw material out of which God can fashion an end result which glorifies Himself.

So take courage.

Take a lot of it!

If your faith seems weak, gain strength in knowing your faith will be greatly fortified as you meet God's functional conditions.

Admit your weakness.

But anticipate God's strength.

Some people have it....
.....some people don't...

3.
The Conscience of a Coward

What do you do if you lack the poise and talent for meeting people well? Does God expect you to make a fool of yourself?

Some people have it. Some people don't.

I don't.

The word is *charisma*, better known as personal magnetism, the special aura encircling those gifted people who can walk into a room and promptly deviate all prior concentrations—and in so doing arouse either the admiration or jealous disdain of everyone present.

Though the word itself had not yet entered my vocabulary, the magic of charisma came to my attention in early childhood as I saw others with exuberant personalities attract attention to themselves.

In addition to being shy, tall and gawky, ugly freckles marred my countenance. Saving coins earned from odd jobs, I responded to an advertisement in a farm magazine and sent off for a jar of Stillman's Freckle Cream, an ointment heralded for its magic in transforming the complexion of faces such as mine. It worked to a limited extent during the winter months, but the sun and wind of spring, as I toiled in the fields of our farm, brought out my speckling in greater profusion than ever.

On many a Sunday morning, faced with the ordeal of attending church and confronting my relentless adversaries, I stood before the partly broken mirror in my bedroom and lamented the uncomely color and contour of my face.

I also gathered together hard-earned money and ordered

31

one of the body-building courses advertised in magazines which came to our home. I even took a correspondence course from Leon See, the trainer of prize-fighter Primo Carnera, who promised to make me the winner of my first bout, whether amateur or professional. Empowered with a "secret punch" taught in the course, I would win the unwavering respect of males my age in town.

After the tenth easy lesson, I talked a reluctant neighbor boy into putting on the gloves. Within five minutes, he bombarded me into humiliating submission!

Among my strengths is an indomitable will—which heightens frustration in the face of failure—and, determined to enhance my personal image, I kept trying other forms of physical development.

But I remained gawky and freckled.

This punitive hangup caused years of delay for an open declaration of spiritual commitment in my life. In the deeps of my person, I wanted a declared relationship with God. But the church I attended emphasized evangelism and, to young males, virility included resistance to Sunday night altar calls; so to avoid compounded ridicule I overtly walked the broad road, hiding the spiritual hunger in my heart.

Some of my cohorts did make the Sunday night trek to the altar. Most, unfortunately, experienced conversion which lasted about as long as Tom Sawyer's revival-meeting episode. Those who stuck experienced a strange metamorphosis. Even the worst of hellions evidenced transformation, as was to be expected, but in the wake of this they seemed to become somewhat effeminate. I remember one chap in particular, a fine athlete who earned considerable plaudits for his prowess. Though he went on to higher achievements following conversion, a strange daintiness characterized his life.

I must have none of that, I reasoned. Add to my slender frame and unglamorous countenance so much as a touch of sissiness and I would forfeit any shelter whatever from the disdain of my oppressors.

Then, after graduating from high school, I enrolled in college. It was, first of all, escape from the doldrums of life in a farming community, but it was also sudden confrontation with a vast horizon of spiritual discovery. Here I met students who equaled and often far exceeded the measurements of those I had considered endowed with the ultimate in physical and personality qualifications back home. Yet, despite their virility, these young men professed and displayed an infectious faith.

"When did you accept the Lord?" Bruce Dunn, now a well-known Presbyterian clergyman, asked me.

"Uh—" I stammered, not only taken back by the question but by the unimpeded naturalness with which he approached me.

The first weekend at Wheaton, I made a public commitment.

For one glorious fortnight I reveled in the conviction that I had not only become an affirmed believer in Christ but, in so doing, had bridged the gap between my timorous past and the robust self-confidence I had so long envied on the part of other young fellows during childhood and adolescence.

Then came reality.

The newly-met stalwarts on the Wheaton campus included a high incidence of those who boldly and consistently witnessed. In contrast to my past, where life in Christ appeared tantamount to lost virility, manliness undergirded the faith of these students.

Painfully I discovered the significant role personal magnetism often plays in Christian witness, how much some Christians equate successful witness with successful merchandising. To their credit, I must say I have met many Christians, endowed with fluorescent personalities, who use their talents to tell others of the reality the Savior has brought into their lives. These Christians exude confidence. They win quick rapport with strangers. They stand out in a crowd. They are born salesmen.

They have charisma.

I have, in fact, met Christians who struck me as being somewhat remiss in many of the important graces of the Christian life who, and it is not for me to question but that they did it sincerely, implemented an enviable knack for talking with other people about the Christian faith.

I met one man some years ago who would accost strangers on the street, on planes and trains. In what seemed to me an uncouth manner, he won the attention, and on occasion the professed conversion, of nonbelievers.

In private life, this man left much to be desired.

He was a whiz in business, running roughshod over competition if necessary to gain his monetary goals, and often gave God the blame for problems he had obviously spawned himself. But a sizable number of converts thank God to this day for his concern and zeal.

On the other side of the coin, I have met people like Bill Portis. We spent several months working together on a film project in Italy, necessitating a good bit of travel together. Bill is the well-educated, well-groomed, executive type, and I recall many times when, permitted a few minutes of encounter with strangers, Bill gave a warm, believable witness. Once, on a train between Rome and Naples, I looked on as he led four men to professed acceptance of Christ, at their request!

Bill had a good swath of progress going for himself in the business world, but he and his wife Shirley shared a restless urge to invest their lives more productively and, as a consequence, did some Christian service apprenticeship in the States, then headed for Italy where Bill works among students and servicemen in Naples in addition to hobnobbing with a lot of interesting people. For instance, he led an Italian film producer to faith a couple of years ago. The man has matured encouragingly as a Christian, opening many subsequent doors of opportunity for this engaging American.

People like me envy guys like Bill.

And with me, as I've indicated, this envy went to seed in my life during that freshman year in college, particularly in the case of a dorm mate. On a campus where both students and faculty members looked upon witnessing as the noblest of endeavors, this chap was the pick of the lot.

Built and countenanced like a professional model, his physique and personality made him a key campus personality, the awe of the girls and the envy of sparsely endowed males such as myself.

I sat many times in wide-eyed hungry-hearted silence as he recounted bold forays against the dominions of darkness. Skid Row or Park Avenue, it didn't seem to matter, he championed infidels as confidently as seekers.

"The gospel is the power of God," he liked to say. "All we have to do is proclaim it."

Often, walking the streets to the place where I worked, I imagined myself emulating his enterprise. I prayed for the courage to do it. But cowardice permeated my mind like a cancer, mocking my prayers, negating every hope and determination.

I might have despaired completely except that on weekends we had what the school called practical work assignments. You might be sent with a half-dozen students to conduct a youth meeting, a downtown rescue-mission service, or perhaps sing and give witness at such institutions as the county jail, the hospital, a home for the aged.

For me, these experiences were like aspirin to someone suffering from chronic headaches. I offered little contribution myself, but being identified with others—and especially on assignments with my prominent and capable dorm mate— gave me a feeling of productive participation in a vital thrust against the forces of darkness.

As Bill McKee puts it, "I was okay playing zone but fell on my face man to man."

Sometimes, often on a completely voluntary basis, we hit the streets armed with gospel tracts. I developed the fastest draw on campus. I could spot a prospect, flip him a copy of *Four Things God Wants You to Know*, and be half a block down the street before you could quote the thirty-fifth verse of John 11.

Then I would see Mr. Personality at work, striking up conversations, warmly and convincingly introducing his witness, tactfully bringing some wanderer to confrontation with spiritual need.

If only I could experience such adventure!

At least once!

About this time Moody Bible Institute's Dr. Will Houghton released his chorus, "Lord, Lead Me to Some Soul Today." We sang it many times. In chapel, in floor devotions. It haunted me throughout the arid months of autumn and winter.

It would be untrue to say I tried, but I surely meant to try.

I read how-to-do-it books on soul-winning, prayed continually for courage, ventured furtively onto the streets, and dared day after day to believe I would draw swords with at least one of the lewd-mouthed unregenerates at work.

But I never did.

I kept faithful with tract distribution, however. I would slip into telephone booths and place tracts in the directories. I left tracts on washbasins, in public lavatories, sneaked them into mailboxes, slipped them under automobile windshield wipers, left them on the seats of streetcars and buses.

Occasionally, when the apex of my courage coincided with the ultimate in my determination, I had hand-to-hand experiences which bolstered my morale. Hand to hand, mind you—passing tracts—not oral witnessing.

During the Christmas holidays, for example, the train

36

homeward stopped for water along the outskirts of a small town. It was the waning years of the depression, and as I looked out the window I saw a vagrant sitting on some railroad ties across two switching tracks.

Like a bolt, the inclination struck me to place in his hands a copy of *Four Things God Wants You to Know*!

But the train had already been halted for several minutes. The man sat some forty or fifty yards away. How could I be sure I could get to him, place the eternal seed into his hands, and scamper back before the train headed on down the track?

Like a daring Daniel, I decided it was worth the impending sacrifice; and so, leaping off the coach, I bounded across the tracks, startling the man by my sudden appearance.

"Excuse me, sir," I said, holding out a copy of the leaflet, "but here is something God wants you to read."

To my delight, he took the tract and looked at it for a curious moment as I glanced back nervously toward the train. Then a smile came to his face. "Say, bud," he said, "I'm mighty grateful to you."

"God bless you, sir," I gasped, the positive note of acceptance quickening my pulse and shortening my breath. "Trust the Lord and I'll see you in heaven someday!"

With that, I turned and hurried back to the coach. Seated again, I glanced out the window. The vagrant was reading.

And I had witnessed to him!

The train started.

I watched.

For as long as I could see him, he continued reading, and for years following I remembered that nameless man in my prayers!

Called upon to address the young people at their weekly meeting in the church back home, I told of my experience, having by this time become considerably proficient in the art of "evangelastics," whereby one embellishes a casual experience with the glitter of spiritual significance. Coming as I did from a small farming community where, in those days, few had the opportunity of college, I, like many an introvert in similar circumstances, emerged from the chrysalis to impressively spread my wings in the presence of those who knew me and loved me and did not cower over me with superior talents.

Once returned to campus, of course, I accepted my diminutive role and played it to the letter.

The advent of spring always brings buoyancy to the human spirit, in my case a renewed resolve to be done with procrastination and to be on with the job. One night, convinced I must do it, I took to the streets alone, out beyond the fringe of the sheltering campus to a residential area leading to a large thoroughfare some two blocks away.

A feeling of dauntlessness came over me.

There would likely be a psych test on the morrow. Latin, too, perhaps. Plus several hours of work remaining on the completion of a bibliography for the term's end paper coming up in freshman rhetoric.

But I must prove to myself I could do it—walk up to a stranger, open a conversation, give my witness, warn him of his need, and draw the net!

Bible in hand, adrenaline flowing freely, hesitant but determined, I strode into the night. Those months of prayer for courage had laid a good foundation upon which my obedience to the call would now structure the edifice of success.

At first the streets were empty, and I comforted myself with the thought of Abraham's willingness to offer Isaac but, at the moment of supreme sacrifice, being spared culmination.

Then, out of the darkness up the street, came the masculine clack of approaching footsteps. Fear knifed in my heart. For a moment, I lost my breath. But I squared my shoulders.

I must not fail.

Out of the reservoir of Bible verses put to memory came the searing admonition of the prophet Ezekiel:

When I say to the wicked, 'You shall surely die'; and you do not warn him or speak out to warn the wicked from his wicked way that he may live, that wicked man shall die in his iniquity, but his blood I will require at your hand. Yet if you have warned the wicked, and he does not turn from his wickedness or from his wicked way, he shall die in his iniquity; but you have delivered yourself. 1

The words were like wind and fire in my thoughts as I fixed my eyes upon the approaching silhouette.

"Ah!" I blurted as the man walked by.

He glanced at me but, preoccupied, did not break his brisk pace.

"Sir—"

I turned, watching him move on into the darkness.

Please help me, God, I prayed silently. *That man might go to hell if I don't do my duty tonight. Please help me.*

I pursued him.

I finally reached him as he stood at the main thoroughfare. I stopped two strides short, unnoticed. The sound of a bus came from up the street. Obviously the man intended to board, a logistical complication I had not anticipated.

I cleared my throat.

The man did not turn and the bus came nearer.

Fear, like acid, destroyed the breath of courage I had summoned moments before.

The Mount Moriah sentiment came over me again. Here I was, willing to talk to a perishing soul. But there, in sharp view now, came the bus he intended to ride. Might it not again be a test of my willingness, having followed him this far but unable to consummate my quest because of his unavailability for dialogue?

Braver soldiers than I, my conscience told me, would intercept his plans, persuade him to forgo the bus ride for a while

Not I!

Such tactics lay beyond the reach of my limited talents. No, I had done my part. I had shown my willingness. God knew my heart.

Once again the words of Ezekiel rose like a cudgel in my thoughts.

"His blood will I require at your hands!"

In the face of all the compounding odds, I felt sure I must talk to this man. There was no circumventing responsibility this time.

"Excuse me, sir!" I ventured.

He turned to me.

He looked me over carefully, perhaps to make sure I wasn't some street hoodlum, and then his eyes fell upon the Bible in my hands, giving me a fragment of courage.

"I'm from the college," I said.

"Yes?"

"Might I ask a personal question?"

He offered no reply.

"I—"

My tongue went numb, my throat dry. The bus loomed imminent now, and the man turned away.

"Please, sir!" I exclaimed.

Once more he turned to me.

"Are you prepared to meet God?" I asked.

"Am I what?" he blurted.

"Do you know the Lord Jesus Christ as your personal Savior?"

There was a moment of enormous silence, broken only by the screech of the bus brakes. Hope rose in my heart. I put my hand into my pocket, fingered a coin, thought how pleasing, how exciting and relatable it would be to ride with him on the bus and explain the claims of the gospel to him.

"Could I—" I began, reaching to touch his arm.

"Get the hell out of here!" he snapped, brushing me aside as he stepped onto the bus.

I have no idea how long I stood there, watching down the street long after the vehicle disappeared from view. I only remember that something died in my heart that night as I numbered myself hopelessly among the spiritually inept, one so handicapped as to be devoid of the talent necessary to perform the spiritual service my heart so yearned to accomplish.

I turned and walked back to the campus, meeting several people, speaking to none of them.

Get the HELL out of here !!......

4.
The Divine Priority

Does the Bible document personal witness as the first priority in a successful Christian life? If so, must the sparsely talented Christian accept this as his inevitable failure pattern?

As a criminal—tormented by his conscience—hides his misdeeds in silence, so I shared my boulevard experience with no one. I continued to go on practical work assignments, profusely passing out tracts, giving my testimony in public meetings, participating in prayer groups where the faithful implored conviction upon the lost and unction upon themselves.

But the spark had gone out.

I saw myself as one who marches in the army of the Lord but fires no rounds at the enemy.

Years passed without my making so much as one overt effort to have a personal encounter with one of the wayward.

Oh, I still tried to consider myself a witness.

During my sophomore year, a sailor stationed in the area joined me in the formation of a successful boys' club at an inner-city church. It was a struggling congregation, so only a handful of participants came from membership families. The majority, pagan kids from off the street, swelled club ranks and offered the most exciting challenge to that point of my Christian life.

These boys hungered for attention, for someone to care about them, and they seemed to look upon the sailor and me as heroes.

It was wonderful.

My introversion sublimated, my personality came into unprecedented flower. To hear me bring one of the brief evangelistic devotionals at the conclusion of an evening's activity, you never would have suspected my reticence on a street corner.

Many of these boys became believers, some of them taking subsequent places of prominence in the work of the church.

Summers I volunteered for counseling at church-sponsored camps. Subsequently two other fellows and I began a camp, renting a Boy Scouts grounds. The camp continues to this day and the present director, a high school science teacher, came to Christ during our first year.

I had the privilege of leading him to faith.

I'm sold on camping, believe it to be one of the most effective tools wielded today by the Christian church. A survey at a leading evangelical college showed a majority of the students on campus either received Christ as Savior or had their decisive spiritual experience at a summer camp.

One of the camps in which I participated lay deep in Appalachia, halfway up the side of a remote hollow which seemed as removed from my natural habitat as the fartherest point on earth. I felt an identification with Hudson Taylor and David Livingstone as, summer after summer, I boarded the train out of Cincinnati and snaked through the hills into true American hinterland.

Religion thrived in the area, and one of the best-known mountain preachers, an illiterate, drew throngs wherever he announced he would speak on his favorite text. The text, which he presumed came from the Bible, was "Every Tub Must Stand on Its Own Bottom."

Though hill folk traipsed to meetings as Chicagoans flock to Wrigley Field when the Cubs have a good year, becoming converted was another matter.

You must feel something.

Hear a voice.

Or see a vision.

44

Otherwise you could not be sure God wanted you in His kingdom.

Consequently, young people at the summer camps where I counseled were rejection prone, especially when they heard the gospel from suspect foreigners like myself. I felt superior to hill folk, I'm ashamed to confess, and whereas at other camps I waited for someone to respond to a campfire message before counseling, here in the hills I occasionally summoned the gumption to corner one of the boys on the subject of his relationship to God.

"Are you a Christian?" I remember asking one.

"I don't reckon," he said.

"Wouldn't you like to be?"

"I s'pect so."

"Now?"

Anticipation quickened my pulse.

But then he shook his head.

Ordinarily this would have sent me off to the volleyball court or for a pensive stroll along the mountain stream which fringed the grounds. But the state of my ego was such that a negative response, rather than cowering me, came as a rebuff.

"Look, pal," I pressured, "the Bible tells us *today is the day of salvation.* We don't know what tomorrow holds. *Boast not yourself of tomorrow, for you know not what a day may bring forth.* God says, *Today if you hear His voice, harden not your heart.*"

Bravo on all those memorized verses, which I reeled off in profusion, my enthusiasm waning somewhat as I saw no particular evidence of awe upon his countenance at my display of evangelical erudition.

"Would you like to receive Christ into your life now?" I asked bluntly.

"Nope," he replied.

"Then when?" I asked.

"When I get a minds to, I reckon," he replied.

I came to loathe that boy.

Workers, as they were called, operated the camp. They were considered missionaries by Northern churches, as much as those who braved the open seas to China, India and Africa. Strongly establishment, sincere though unskilled in the ways of good camping, they emphasized hard-sell evening evangelistic services.

I spoke frequently, elated when some made open profession of faith.

Backsliding was the scourge of the hollows, however. I did not make any in-depth study, but I suspect it was a part of the theology. To remain true in unbroken continuity, it seemed, was to deny one's human failing. So most believers backslid, some catapulting farther downward than others. But there were those who, even in the teeth of opposition, faithfully staked out loyalty to the gospel as it was proclaimed by those of us who came from "up yonder."

Camps in the North were different.

At a camp just inside the Wisconsin border above Chicago, where I had my first exposure to week-long evangelism in the out-of-doors, an excellent program proved conducive to building rapport with boys in attendance and, as a result, experiencing the opportunity of one-to-one witness.

I will always remember the day a boy came to me and asked to be shown how to believe. It was a fantastic experience!

Opening my Bible, taking him verse by verse over the procedure I had so well learned but so rarely employed, I literally saw the light of credence come to his eyes.

Through the years I have run across several who, as campers, were either strongly influenced spiritually or came to a definite knowledge of Christ as a result of my witness. For example, I found one managing an equipment rental office where we secured specialized items for motion-picture production. I came upon another serving as a customs officer in an airport where I often enter the U.S. from overseas assignments. One man, now a successful pastor, amazed me when he told me only a couple of years ago, "You led me to Christ at Camp Shagbark. I will always be grateful." I, frankly, had forgotten the occasion.

With rare exceptions, these and others who came to Christ in camps where I counseled, and who remain true to the faith as adults, were part of a similar pattern. I had looked after them during their daily activities, shepherded them at night while they slept, but their commitment to Christ did not result from my initiative but as the result of the influence of the camp itself, particularly group meetings.

I might have settled for this kind of low-profile participation in spiritual harvest, were it not that, as the years passed, I frequently met Christians for whom the experience was glowingly different. Salesmen, engineers, professional people, daily wage earners, all of them blessed with that special knack for touching the life of another individual and, through that touch, becoming instrumental in the miracle of transformation.

Dick Hillis, with whom I traveled in China, stresses strongly the role of the church, not in evangelism, as is usually supposed, but as a stimulator of evangelists. "We must work with the church," he says, "until witnessing by its members becomes spontaneous, automatic, continuous and contagious, and until results appear with monotonous regularity. For this we need to be sensitive to the Holy Spirit's guidance of how and where."

I'm a candidate for this!

But somehow, I reasoned, I had developed immunity against such blessed endeavors. Compounding my natural inferiority complex was a spiritual inferiority complex.

I never became complacent about my paucity of witness, however, and I'm grateful for that. I think this is indicative of something I amplify later. I was a man with a burden, concerned about widespread disinterest in the church, aware of the lostness of the people around me. I saw the world as a great den of iniquity—careening toward judgment—and the faithful, such as myself, citizens of a better land who would one day gain reward for remaining true to the cause.

That was it!

True to the cause!

In this dark world of woe, I might not be able to rescue many from the pit but, through the silent spectacle of my faithfulness, I could remind men of the gospel.

"People know where I stand"—that timeworn evangelical dodge for failing to witness—became a part of my vocabulary.

Then, too, shortly after marriage, writing consumed more and more of my time. Encouraged by editors such as Ted Engstrom, Bob Walker and Laurin Zorn, I soon began supporting myself and our growing family with free-lance income.

After the China experience, evangelical—often evangelistic—fervor permeated my writing, resulting in reports of lives touched by my literary efforts.

What molten bliss to a yearning heart!

A young mother told me of her child, stricken with leukemia. Concerned for the welfare of his soul, she tried to guide him to faith. But he couldn't seem to understand the gospel.

"I was getting desperate," she told me. "Then a friend gave me your book, *Winky Lost in the Rockies*. Terry loved the story. When we reached the end of the book, where Winky becomes a Christian, he told me he understood. Just before he died, he assured me he knew without a doubt he was going to heaven!

I wept.

A soldier picked up something I had written in the tent of an officer, was converted as a result, and wrote to tell me about it.

People know where
I stand.....

A teenager, in open rebellion against her parents, received one of my books as a gift, refused to read it at first, then browsed one day, subsequently read the entire book, and as a result experienced transforming conversion.

"I was a rank unbeliever," a man in his early twenties told me following a church service where I spoke. "My mother gave me a couple of your books as a gift. I'm crazy about reading, didn't have anything else handy, so looked over one of them. I got interested, disgusted when I came to the first religious part, but kept on reading. I liked the book so well I read it a second time, then a third time. Each time I read it, I got a little more into the religious part, and before I knew what was happening, the gospel message had really grabbed my heart, and I got converted."

Stories of mine began to appear in magazines, weekly Sunday school papers. They were dramatized on radio broadcasts. Letters came as a result, reporting conversions.

I felt a sense of relief.

My lips might be closed but my typewriter spoke with a clarion voice.

For years I quieted my qualms with this assumption.

God did shower my life with many blessings, chief among them being the beginning years of a most enriching marriage.

Before the birth of our first child, my wife and I determined to establish a Christian home where love and good communications would set the climate for spiritual discovery.

God has honored that aspiration.

While we make no claims of perfection, all of our seven children embrace the Christian faith, each of them brought to commitment by either my wife or me at the individual child's request.

We never pushed conversion. In each case, it came with complete naturalness. Was this not the fullest measure of witness, I reasoned, leading one's own flesh to the walk of faith?

It disturbs me to hear of Christian families where children become wayward, for it seems to me if parents live by the admonition in the first four verses of Ephesians 6, commitment should be inevitable. I especially wonder about parents who evangelize other people's offspring but neglect their own!

Success with my typewriter flourished.

My novel *Shadows Under the Midnight Sun* set records in those days for quantity sales. A children's book grew into an adventure series. And magazine acceptances became increasingly easy to come by.

I had visions of grandeur. I could serve God in the seclusion of my study, enjoy reasonable financial success, live the truly good life.

But that was when the telephone rang and Bob Pierce, founder of the World Vision organization, asked if I would go with him on his second trip to China, cover the event for religious magazines, and also do a book.

Although we were in the middle of arrangements for moving to a new house and had a demanding brood of tots, my wife gave enthusiastic approval.

Bob and I traversed China from Peking to Canton and from Shanghai to Kunming.

Graciously, this enormously talented man let me take many engagements which he could have filled, speaking to student groups. The spiritual interest shown by those students, and the suffering and deprivation I witnessed in the wake of the revolutionary struggle in the land, stimulated me as nothing had ever done.

I went to China a young free-lance writer, earning a good income with my typewriter and dreaming dreams of pious affluence. I left China a changed man, with subsequent decisions in my life to be predicated on the China experience and, to God's glory, enhanced accordingly.

Chinese Christians demonstrated an implementation of the Christian faith completely new to my experience.

I met those who had been buried alive, given the water treatment, those who had seen loved ones tortured, even crucified. Yet their faith remained undaunted.

Mr. Lee, a wealthy exporter in Tientsin, lingers to this day as an indelible memory. His home was right out of a Pearl Buck novel. Materially, he was one of the haves in the midst of a nation of have-nots. But his greatest wealth lay not in bank balances, in a land where inflation had grown to nightmare proportions, but in his Christian faith.

Only an American military presence kept Tientsin free. The train Bob and I took down from Peking had, a few nights before, been blown off the track by Maoist infiltrators. When we left Tientsin, we flew over a bivouac of several thousand Red troops.

Refugees left the port of Tientsin in droves—by ship, by junk, even by Chinese sampans. The privileged fled by air. For the fall of the city loomed imminent.

"When are you leaving?" I asked Mr. Lee as we sat at tea one afternoon in his garden.

"We are much too busy this summer," he said. "My wife and I won't be taking a holiday."

"I wasn't thinking of a holiday," I said. "When are you leaving Tientsin permanently?"

He put down his teacup and looked me full in the eyes.

"We aren't leaving Tientsin," he said. "We are staying right here."

A thousand questions congested my thoughts. Even the most optimistic gave the city no more than six months of freedom. From his substantial earnings, Mr. Lee gave vast sums each year to spiritual causes. He could have purchased one of the DC3s airlifting refugees to Formosa and Korea.

Surely his name stood high on Mao's list. To remain meant certain death.

"You seem surprised," he said, smiling when the silence lingered.

"Why are you staying?" I managed to say.

Mr. Lee reflected for a moment, then told me how he and his wife had made their decision after much thought and prayer. Plainly, it had not been an easy decision.

"I have approximately two hundred people employed in my business," he said. "Only a few of them are Christians. I am giving my personal witness, whenever and whatever way I can, to the others. But they look at me, and I know what is in their thoughts. I can speak of the Christian faith, they reason, knowing I will be able to escape before Mao's troops take over here."

He grew silent again.

I waited tensely.

"You will soon be back in America," he continued slowly. I sensed no trace of envy in his voice. "One day you will read in your papers that Tientsin has fallen. When you do, promise to pray much for me, because those will be my days of greatest opportunity. Then my associates will see the sincerity of my witness. But the time may be very short, with much to be accomplished. Be sure to pray for me!"

Tientsin fell.

I was in and out of Hong Kong several times the next few years, and tried to unearth word of Mr. Lee's fate. No information quite pinpointed specifics. But I did learn that the pastor of the Methodist church the Lees attended was put to death together with several members of the congregation. Very likely Mr. Lee died with them.

Shortly after returning from the Orient, and specifically because of the impact the Orient had had upon my life, I participated in the organization of the Gospel Films ministry in Muskegon, Michigan, and have been in the production of Christian films ever since. It is hard work and my second love, writing being much more to my temperament and preference.

But films in the church were avant-garde in those days and I sensed a widening horizon for easy-does-it witness.

Jack Sonneveldt, prominent Grand Rapids businessman, was among the laymen who organized the ministry and served for several years as the organization's president. A warm friendship developed between us but, because Jack consistently and effectively gave his witness to the people he contacted in his associations, I felt rebuked many times by his zeal.

"Even though we are involved in public Christian ministry," Jack warned, "we must always remember one thing. The films we make are important, but they must never serve as an excuse for neglecting personal witness. It's the same with being active in the church. Nothing can take the place of personal witness."

His words were like a heel blister to one such as I wearing the comfortable shoes of religious activity. Curtailing most of my free-lance writing for motion-picture production, I plunged into the writing of scripts and the direction of films, a number of which caught on quite well.

Seventeen had a far-reaching ministry, in multitudes of churches and in hundreds of high schools. Youth for Christ director Gene McGee, for example, screened the film in nearly every public school assembly of metropolitan Chicago.

The film *Centerville Awakening*, a cry out of my own searching heart, was reputed to have been shown in more churches in its first two years than any evangelical film previously released.

"It must be wonderful, Ken," my friends said, many of them perhaps enviously, "to know you are reaching so many people."

If only they could see the inner reaches of my heart!

Without question I was serving God. But was I serving Him in full obedience? Was my witness clear? Did it please Him?

It took a family crisis to face me head on with the answer to my questions.

These were the years prior to the emergence of Jonas

57

Salk, and one summer a raging polio epidemic swept our community. Of those afflicted, one in ten died, including the neighbor girl.

Two of our sons contracted the disease and were placed in hospital quarantine. We carefully watched over the others, alert for the slightest symptom.

After ten days, we decided it would be feasible for me to take an appointment about one hundred miles away. After I arrived at my destination, however, I received a telephone call from my wife. Our oldest daughter had a fever and stiffening of the neck muscles. The doctor was on his way to our house.

I jumped into the car and sped homeward. To my surprise and momentary relief, as I entered the house, our daughter lay on the living room couch.

"She begged the doctor to let her stay until you got back," my wife whispered.

Our daughter was nine, a treasure to both of us, her sensitive spirit and imaginative resourcefulness a shining joy in our household. But never had she been so radiant as that day.

She reached out her hands, touching her mother with one and me with the other. She told us she loved us. She thanked us for the love we had shown to her. She asked forgiveness for little abrasions she had caused. She told us not to worry, because she was sure of her faith.

In the event we might not see her again, once she entered quarantine, she told us what part of the Bible she would like read at her funeral, a special song she wanted sung.

There were tears in her eyes—not to mention ours!—but she maintained control of herself. I thanked God. This little life was truly in His hands, and it was surely because my wife and I had tried to make the Christian faith relevant to her.

Several weeks later, after all three children had safely returned home from the hospital and were well advanced in therapeutic procedures, the full impact of what our daughter had contributed to my life got through to me.

It happened as I sat one evening reading the book of Acts, the opening scene prior to Christ's ascension. High excitement electrified the disciples. With their Master's resurrection, what had appeared to be the dismal defeat of Calvary vanished like darkness at the rise of the morning sun. Surely the Architect of creation, who had become the lowly Carpenter of Nazareth, was about to set Himself up on earth as King of kings and Lord of lords.

Why did He delay?

More than a month had passed since the morning He came upon them in the room where they had securely locked the doors against the hostile world. Even Thomas believed that morning, in the face of evidence too awesome for disbelief.

A month is a long time when one remains in the throes of mediocrity in full anticipation of imminent transcendence. So, restless, it appears likely from the Acts text that the disciples began to scheme among themselves. Matthew might have voiced his intent to be the ruler of Egypt. Physician Luke, they may have reasoned, could be master of the land of Hippocrates and have his governmental seat in Athens. Peter, of course, would reign in Rome. Let restless Thomas, with legions of angels at his command, venture eastward in the exploration of new domains.

Like many of us who have followed their example, they went to Jesus with their plan.

"Lord," they asked, *"is it at this time You are restoring the kingdom of Israel?"* 1

What they were really saying was, "Lord, we want to make it big. We want to put down the Roman Empire, rule the world, have all the facilities of earth at our command. All for Your glory, Lord! Understand that, of course!"

A look of intense pain must surely have come to the Savior's countenance, and at first they wondered why.

"It is not for you to know times or epochs," He said. *"But you shall receive power when the Holy Spirit has come upon you; and you shall be My witnesses both in Jerusalem, and in all Judea and Samaria, and even to the remotest part of the earth."* 2

Then, before they could offer rebuttal, He lofted heavenward, a cloud receiving Him out of their sight.

The truth of what happened here came upon me with force.

Our daughter had thought she might be talking to her mother and me for the last time. Naturally, then, she poured from her heart the most important words of her life—her love for us, the sureness of her faith.

Jesus, of course, knew He was making His final earthly utterance to the disciples. Doesn't it seem logical that He would speak the most significant words of His entire ministry—words appropriate for believers of that time, words appropriate for believers today?

Witnesses!

That's what Jesus wanted.

That's what He still wants.

"Lord," I prayed, "if You can use a coward to make Your grace known to lost men, then please use me!"

I had prayed that prayer in essence before. Now I prayed with a whisper of hope in my heart. I was to be my Lord's witness, but He promised to give me the strength to do it.

Perhaps, at last, the strength to rise above my detested cowardice!

5.
Color It Yellow

Does effective witness depend upon a gift of gab? Are only the qualified expected to speak?

Evangelist Jack Wyrtzen says, "When it comes to witness, silence isn't golden, it's yellow!"

His words catch me right between the eyes.

Yellow is to cowards what red, white and blue are to heroes.

Anyone who knows Jack Wyrtzen is aware of the charismatic glow of his personality. Tireless in his spiritual efforts, head of an organization mushrooming in influence across the world, Jack is nonetheless never too busy for personal witness. It may be someone he meets casually, a salesman calling at his office, or contact with a celebrity through one of the radio or television talk shows on which he frequently and effectively appears. To all, with equal concern and genuineness, he elucidates the Christian faith.

Numbering Jack among my cherished friends, thus closely aware of his concern for personal witness on the part of all Christians, I'm sure he leveled his statement at those who shun responsibility, who, as was so long my case, use inability as an excuse for noninvolvement. Though admittedly endowed with a flair for salesmanship and promotion, I'm also sure he is just as vulnerable to the temptation of silence as many other Christians.

So am I saying that God expects you to be able to articulate the gospel with Jack Wyrtzen's ease and eloquence?

Ease or eloquence in witnessing is not the issue.

What then?

If it kills us, God expects you and me to daily hit the streets, buttonhole passersby, warn them of the wrath to come as we extol the anticipations of heaven?

Perhaps.

But then again, perhaps not.

Let me share with you the premise which helped me get off dead center on the subject, a premise talented envoys such as Jack Wyrtzen would heartily endorse.

For me, the springboard to an approach to witnessing compatible to cowards lay in John 15 where Jesus said, *"I am the vine, you are the branches; he who abides in Me, and I in him, the same bears much fruit; for apart from Me you can do nothing."*[1]

Put into plain Monday-through-Saturday English, our Lord tells us the burden of proof in witnessing lies on His shoulders, not on ours!

Get this fact solemnly and securely anchored to your fear problem, and you will find yourself facing up to the mainstream of a Christian's responsibility and opportunity rather than drifting downstream into the jagged rocks of discouragement and embarrassment.

God doesn't ask you and me to work for Him. He asks us to let Him do His work through us.

"We are His workmanship," the Bible tells us, *"created in Christ Jesus for good works."* [2] I'm only a marginal Bible student at best when it comes to exegesis, but that reads to me as though God fashioned me to be an instrument of His rather than an independent operator on my own. I am part of a plan, not a loner, a design instead of a happenstance.

I once heard a Bible teacher suggest the word *Christian* means "Little Christ."

Beautiful!

In His sublime prayer, recorded in John 17, Jesus asked for His disciples—including the Baptists, Methodists, Lutherans, Presbyterians and those of sundry alignment—that they may understand their mission in life.

"They are not of the world," Christ implored His Father, *"even as I am not of the world. Sanctify them in the truth.... As Thou didst send Me into the world, even so have I sent them into the world."* 3

Sent for what?

To continue what Christ came to instigate: the proclamation of a transforming faith.

Then we are to continue the work of Christ Himself?

Precisely!

And you would think for a moment this could be done in the energy of humanness, however gifted that human might be?

Impossible!

Then how?

Remember the promise of the first chapter of Acts? Jesus said, *"You shall receive power when the Holy Spirit has come upon you; and you shall be My witnesses."*

When shall you be a witness?

When the Holy Spirit has come upon you!

Don't see God through the distorted lenses some people wear. He isn't the dominant father image, a policeman who looks down upon the world and tabulates our many demerits so he can hold them against us on judgment day.

God is on our side, and estrangement comes by our lack of trust in Him, not by His rejection of us.

You are not a happenstance inhabitant of planet earth, but a special creation of God for a specific purpose ordained by Him. The tragedy of earth is not essentially its ecological problems, its social iniquities, its deadly political games, but the failure of individual men—from plebes to presidents—to realize that God placed every human being on earth for the purpose of glorifying Him.

See yourself in this perspective. You will then understand that witnessing isn't some kind of penance you do to appease an angry God. You don't need an overdosed guilt complex for motivation. Converting men isn't like shooting clay pigeons, with a prize going to the most proficient marksmen.

No, witnessing is being available to God.

It is obedience.

You must come to grips with the awesome realization that God needs you. Call it cliché, but your lips and your hands and your feet are the only lips and hands and feet God has to do His work on this earth.

About the time these concepts began getting through to me, I came into the realization of what the Bible talks about in the one hundredth psalm when it says, *"Know that the Lord Himself is God; it is He who has made us, and not we ourselves."* 4

I am convinced effective soul-winners are never self-made.

They are always God-made!

God does not expect you to generate courage and enthusiasm for witnessing. He is not dependent upon your cleverness, your way with people, your gift of gab. He isn't a statistician who blesses you if you are batting over .300 and sends you back to the minors if you fall into a slump.

Oh, He wants to utilize your talents, to be sure, which is the whole point. A valid disciple of Jesus Christ isn't someone who somehow succeeds in reverting to the id state, becoming a kind of flesh-and-blood robot.

Quite the contrary.

We are laborers together with God, remember?

Now, of course, a farmer doesn't say, "I'm going to go out into the field this morning and work in fellowship with my tractor." A baseball player doesn't say, "My bat and I have developed such a harmonious association, I am consistently able to clout the ball over the left-field fence."

Being a tool in God's hand does not relegate you to the status of hammers and brooms.

Prior to conversion, you were a citizen of this world. Faith, the Bible tells us, immediately numbered you among *"strangers and exiles on the earth."* 5

"This world is not my home," the song writer penned, "I'm just passing through."

Consequently, your relationship to God rises above earthly definitions. Being a tool in God's hand immediately presupposes transcendence. The word implies humility in the same breath in which it denotes service.

Let me try to give you a handle you can grab hold of. As I have come to understand it, an effective witness is one who does exert initiative, who does prepare himself and who learns from failure and success, but whose efforts at all times center in the realization that he must depend upon God for his guidance, his motivation, his implementation, and his subsequent effectiveness in telling others about the reality of Jesus Christ.

The issue, then, is not whether or not I am a coward—I am!—but whether or not I understand the procedure God has ordained, the only procedure whereby anyone may adequately dispense the truth of the gospel to a world steeped in spiritual error.

We live in an age of multiexploration into the meaning of the Holy Spirit.

Wonderful!

What a sorry plight the church would be in if we had no believers seeking to understand the role of the Holy Spirit and the meaning of an experience blessed by His presence and energy.

Perhaps you will find empathy in a confession I have had to make. For years, I resisted the full flow of the Holy Spirit in my life. I didn't want to. But being conservative by nature, I somehow couldn't see myself in fraternity with believers, many of them my good friends, who professed to have had a lightning-strike experience with the Holy Spirit.

Yet, thirsting for visible fruition in my Christian life, I secretly sought the mystical touch. I wore the pages thin around the area of 1 Corinthians 12 in my study Bible, at times expectant, more often apprehensive of what could happen.

Might I one day speak with a tongue of fire, lay hands on a sick man and see him instantaneously restored, utter prophecies, behold visions? I cringed at the thought of it—and felt deeply convicted, aware that I was in fact fighting against God's right to let the Holy Spirit do His work within my heart, in whatever manner that work might be expressed.

One day I received a telephone call from the pastor of one of those churches known for demonstrative modes of worship.

"We have several of your books in our church library, Brother Ken," he said, "and although we don't show motion pictures in our church, a number of our people have seen your films at Youth for Christ. We would like to have you speak at our evening service some Sunday night."

My first impulse was to refuse. But my conscience wouldn't let me. Hadn't I asked God for His will in every facet of my life? Couldn't I trust Him to send my way the encounters needed to shape my life into the image of His design? Perhaps among these people, who claimed to do exploits through the power of the Holy Spirit, I might find the rainbow's end to my search.

"I'll be happy to come to your church, Pastor," I said.

It was a delightful experience.

The singing had a lilt and glory which lifted my heart, and I sensed a freedom and exuberance in the meeting strangely and refreshingly different from other congregations.

The pastor bothered me some. Defense mechanism may have caused me to misjudge him, but he seemed quite egotistical. He led the entire meeting—or so it seemed—interspersed songs and the testimony time and announcements with deft reminders of his own importance. The way he introduced me didn't improve my attitude toward him.

"As Brother Ken speaks to us, folks," he said, "keep in mind that, as far as I can tell, he has yet to experience the fullness of the Holy Spirit in his life, but he is a good brother, he loves the Lord, and I'm sure he'll be a blessing."

Apparently I was a specimen, brought in to document the aridness of a soul inside the kingdom, but astray from its green pastures. I somehow stumbled through a brief discourse.

"We'll be praying for you, Brother Ken," the pastor said as I headed homeward some forty minutes later.

He offered no honorarium for my services, but that often happens. Had he done so, the money would have gone into a special fund for overseas student evangelism. It was payment enough to have another alibi for resisting the Holy Spirit's claim upon my life, and I succeeded for several days in putting the subject out of mind.

Eventually, however, I came back again and again to 1 Corinthians 12, and the prior tug and twisting of my conscience reactivated.

Wasn't I the type with an aversion to fixation thinking? Then why let one man, this pastor, validate my disinclinations to zealotry? What about those fine examples of the Pentecostal persuasion I had met before? Did they indeed possess something I refused to claim for myself?

One day, tired of it all, I determined to throw my heart and life open to whatever the Holy Spirit wanted to perform in me. It was a terrifying decision. But I knew I had to do it.

"Lord," I prayed, "if there is anything the Holy Spirit needs to do in my life which hasn't been done, so I can experience the fullness You have for me, I no longer resist it."

A reverent hush came upon me, a quietness, a tranquillity— like the stillness of air across a countryside prior to the inrush of stormy weather.

And then what happened?

Did I speak in tongues?

No.

Did I see a vision?

No.

69

But I felt as though an enormous load had been hoisted from my chest!

Don't ask me to explain the logistics of my experience.

I can't.

I do know I underwent a realization of reciprocal possessiveness which was new and wonderful to my heart. Christ was mine, in all His redeeming and empowering majesty, and I was His, in my weakness and cowardice, to be sure, but only as weakness and cowardice were touched by His power.

Since that day, I no longer criticize those who lay claim to the Pentecostal experience. Frankly, my taste in evangelists leans more toward Billy Graham, Barry Moore or John Haggai, but I'm quick to defend Oral Roberts when he is criticized in my presence. I am now convinced the work of the Holy Spirit in a believer's heart is a decisive experience, and it is not for me to discredit those who, in sincerity, claim to have had overt manifestations in contrast to my quiet victory.

The issue is this: Because of my sick ego, my rebellion, I had been afraid of the possibilities.

Afraid of what?

Of reality?

I began to go back and pick up some of the pieces over the long trail of my search. They fit together beautifully, no longer like a jigsaw puzzle but like a resplendent mosaic.

I took special note of one item.

No matter how despondent I had become in the past over my failure as a witness, I never lost the desire to witness.

This is important, a vital key.

I remembered the morning when I flew with MAF pilot Don Robertson across the rolling hills of Honduras. Don, an exceptionally fine pilot, subsequently lost his life in a plane crash, but I do not question the tragic event because of the concept Don shared with me that morning as we flew from Teguciagalpa to the base at Siguatepeque.

We were talking about the will of God, how elusive it seems to be to some Christians, yet how futile Christian effort is unless we are sure of it.

"I always think of what David wrote in the thirty-seventh psalm," Don said above the roar of the engine. "God told him, *'Delight yourself in the Lord; and He will give you the desires of your heart.'* 6

I listened intently.

"As I've come to understand that verse," Don continued, "we are not told God will give us our hearts' desires. What God is promising is to put into our hearts the desires we should have to glorify Him. Then, as we grow in our spiritual lives, He gives us the strength and guidance to fulfill those desires, thus performing His will for us."

It all began to come clear to me now. I had had my preconceived image of what a witnessing Christian should be like. I had to somehow fill that niche or fail.

Wrong!

Clifford Lewis is a cherished friend of mine, and such a relentless and effective witness, but I am not Clifford Lewis. While he lived, I heard many messages from the lips of Dr. Walter Wilson, but I am not Dr. Walter Wilson. Bill Bright's enthusiasm for personal witness has cascaded into the enormously effective Campus Crusade movement, but I am not Bill Bright.

I am Ken Anderson.

A coward.

But I have learned that God meets us at the point of our need. My need is for courage, for guidance around my inbred reluctance, and God meets me at this point of need.

I don't question but what some people need visible excitement in their spiritual experience.

Fine.

My temperament best fits what God talks about when He says, *"In quietness and confidence shall be your strength,"* 7 a promise which sticks to my ribs like well-turned filet!

71

So the way to victory is quietness for all believers?

Quite obviously not.

Del Kingswriter, Assembly of God missionary in East Africa, has become a man of recognized stature among missionaries and nationals alike and is one of my most appreciated friends. Del, a specialist in audiovisual communications, worked with us on the production of *Between Two Worlds*, our first student evangelism film for Africa.

We're both joggers and every morning before breakfast we did a brisk mile together. Nights, after dinner, we'd stroll down quiet Nairobi boulevards, talk about the day's filming and the coming schedule and, inevitably, share our joy in Christ.

"The Holy Spirit is very real in my life, Ken," Del said, "but I can certainly see He is just as real in your life. I cannot ally myself with those in our movement who feel we have an exclusive corner on the work of the Holy Spirit."

Del is quick to admit phonies invade the Pentecostal camp.

So?

We liturgists aren't without an Achan and an Ananias singing the doxology on Sunday morning!

What a refreshing day it would be if Christians could stick with the issues. Instead of trying to win others to our particular viewpoint, let's be in unity on the dynamic premise that God is God and He wants to fit us into just one mold— that pattern of His specific will for each of us as individuals.

I've been a prime target for many well-meaning Christians who wanted to see me grow the kind of feathers displayed by their particular flock. They have sent me tape recordings, magazine subscriptions, reams of mimeographed verifications of the allegedly special way.

One well-meaning soul gave me a manual of instructions on how, by repeating in rhythm such combinations as "x-z, x-z, x-z, q-b, q-b, j-t, j-t," I would liberate my tongue and be swept into the ecstatic language of the fully anointed.

72

I'm convinced that in this matter of the filling of the Holy Spirit there is a unity of experience but a diversity of expression. And the rudimentary test in the final analysis is found in Paul's exhortation to the First Church of Galatia, to whom he said, *"The fruit of the Spirit is love, joy, peace, patience, kindness, goodness, faithfulness, gentleness, self-control; against such there is no law."* 8

I've made a lot of mistakes in my life, but I'm so thankful God helped me to keep the faith as a witness until I understood, with at least some clarity, how He intended to work through me in spite of my weaknesses.

How does this work on behalf of those of us who have admitted to cowardice? We'll explore this fully later on, but here is a bit of foretaste.

Bob Cook, president of Kings College, pinpointed procedure for me when he said one day, "Ken, I'm trying to relate every event of my life to my privileges and responsibilities as a child of God. When the telephone rings, I put my hand on it for a moment while I breathe a prayer for guidance, asking God to use me in any way He can to minister to the person whose identity I do not yet know. When I board an airplane, I ask for guidance as to the seat I should take. When someone occupies a seat next to me, I ask God for the wisdom to represent Him in the way He would have me to do. I just don't believe we have any business trying to serve God unless we are willing to let Him handle the strategy. He is God, you know, and the more we learn how to let God be God in our lives, the more effective we will be as His representatives."

The key word is *availability*.

When I awaken in the morning, I tell God I'm available for the purpose He has for my life that day. I ask Him to send across my path those whom I can help and, conversely, to bring my way those who can be of help to me. When I travel, when some salesman or local businessman comes to my office, wherever I am, my prayer is, "Lord, here I am. I don't savvy much, and You know how short I am on courage, but I'll do what You show me to do. If You want me to witness to someone, open the conversation so I can do it. If no opportunity comes, then I'll be content to know that You had nothing special for me to do or, perhaps, You permitted me to bear witness in some silent way."

Please understand me. I am enough concerned about genuineness in the Christian life not to take this kind of approach as salve for a sensitive conscience. I want to be an effective witness. I wish I could be as effective as some of my friends, but I am not one of my friends. I'm me. And I'm convinced God never vitally uses any of my friends, never uses any Christian, and surely never uses me, unless we fully depend upon Him for guidance.

So let's package it this way: if you tend to be tight-lipped in this witness business, take courage. Of course, it could be you need to play square with God in the matter of spiritual cleanliness. If so, do it! But it could also be that you need to come into the aura of understanding how God intends to use you, how He has provided resources for you to serve Him.

The silence of a coward who just plain refuses to witness is most assuredly yellow. But the silence of a Christian genuinely seeking guidance in the right way of witness is golden with the promise of fulfillment.

6.
Be Your Own Best Customer

Witness is both ideology and theology, outreach to others but also "inreach" to yourself, as you learn how to make spiritual ideas productive in your experience.

Psychologists, ever searching the mind of man to determine why we do the things we do, now suggest that many of our problems are rooted in the fact that we hate ourselves. We cannot truly care about others until we begin caring about ourselves.

At first encounter, those words sound grossly incongruous.

What about ego-tripping?

Vanity, self-pampering, with all their ramifications, may well stem from this inner dislike of ourselves which then motivates various forms of ego as a futile effort to pretend to be what we are not but would be pleased and proud if we were.

Looking back across the vistas of my own life, I see much evidence of this self-hatred. I detest incompetence in no one so much as I detest it in myself. Not until I finally came to see this guy Ken Anderson as someone God fashioned for His own special purpose—in fact, a unique and strategic creation—did I begin to understand how much reticence and fear are attributes of carnality, and rarely, if ever, virtuous.

This, then, maps out new terrain for stalking down cowardice.

First of all, before you can convince someone else of the validity of the gospel, you must convince yourself.

You must be your own best customer.

75

This does not imply doubting your salvation. As you well know, salvation depends entirely upon the grace and mercy of God through Jesus Christ. Regeneration occurs only as a man cries out from the mire of his own hopelessness, recognizing his total inability to merit or manipulate an answer to his need.

We are considering, instead, what happens to a Christian when he not only knows he has experienced salvation but when this experience, as God intended it to be, continually matures into a full and productive life. *"As you therefore have received Christ Jesus the Lord,"* the Bible tells us, *"so walk in Him."* [1]

Let's suppose the psychologist is right and we do hate ourselves. Then we must see the love of God made relevant to self-appraisal, and see such evidence of transforming power in our own experience that we must share the experience with others.

"I'm a beautiful person!"

A statement of vanity?

Not if you also say, "Beautiful because the beauty of Jesus is seen in me!"

Let me once again become confessional.

You have had a look into the gulley of sparse confidence in my life. Now let me tell you about bridges.

I have never been to a psychiatrist, though I respect the work they do. The human mind is a highly complex instrument which makes the most sophisticated computer look like an early Burroughs.

One outstanding parapsychologist, awed at the enormous capacity of the human brain, has suggested the possibility of a child coming into the world with a mind which already has programmed into it the total knowledge of all time and space, learning being the process of unearthing this resource.

Though I cannot conceive of such conjecture being plausible, it surely is an intriguing one and suggests, by its very postulation, the vast floor space of man's cranial cavity.

What I do believe is that the mind is the arena of all reality in human experience. Solomon, considering the mind of man, wrote, *"As he thinketh in his heart, so is he."* 2

Borrowing the existentialist's pen for a moment, one might also state, "As a man thinks, so things are."

I reject the sentimentalism so often associated with the heart. True, the human breast experiences emotional sensations, but I believe the stimulus emanates solely from the brain. In moments of extreme insecurity, I experience sharp pain at the base of my spine, but no one can convince me that any aspect of consciousness resides there.

The intellect, the emotions, the will, the personality—plus spiritual consciousness!—all have their habitat in the head. Transplantation of human organs, including the heart, is solely therapeutical. Brain transplants could only occur if God permitted man to put his finger on the button marked Genesis.

Properly trained and disciplined, the mind is capable of fantastic performance. Neglected and misused, it can be a man's biggest problem. What needs to happen, quite obviously, is for one to learn how to make his mind work for him instead of against him.

The Bible poses a list of interesting options involving the mind. It says, *"Let this mind be in you, which was also in Christ Jesus."* 3

Such a statement seems so superlative as to be completely in the realm of eternal anticipation, not temporal adaptation. I read the verse many times, was profoundly bothered by it. Whatever was the Bible trying to say? Could I, earthbound with so many limitations, literally attain the mentality of Jesus?

Absurd.

Then one day, chatting with Jack Sonneveldt about the complexities of the Christian experience, he made a statement which lit a fire in my heart. We had been talking about the first two verses of Romans 12 as God's pattern for true commitment, and Jack said, "I've heard a lot of sermons on those two verses, but there is one little phrase in there that bugs me. It's the phrase *'by the renewing of the mind.'* Have you ever heard a sermon on that?"

I hadn't.

"I'd walk fifty miles to hear one!" Jack said.

By the renewing of the mind! One translation puts it, *"Let the Holy Spirit remake you from the inside."*

I believe God is talking about our learning to think as Christians, for surely no one can properly act like a Christian until he has learned to think like a Christian. And by "act" we dare not presume ecclesiastical performance. Instead, learning to act like a Christian involves the total self and all its relationships in harmony with Jesus Christ, thus qualifying for witness because lost men see standing in my shoes the evidence of transformation.

The more I mulled over the phrase *by the renewing of the mind*, the more it intrigued me. I saw my shallowness, my martyr complex, the child in me so often supplanting the adult. And, above all, my natural bent to cowardice!

The phrase remained academic to me for some time but, the more I thought about it, the more my attitude changed—to inquisitiveness, to longing, to at times yearning anticipation.

I talked to no one, but a seed had been sown which I determined to see nurtured to full oak. I knew that to become an effective witness there had to be a ring of genuineness to my own experience.

Sure, I knew Christ; I fled to Him often in moments of need. But I had not yet discovered Him as the Giver of abundant life, the Fulfiller of personality, the one who can touch the ordinary, even the presumed mediocre, and give meaning and value. But how did one go about this renewing?

I remembered what Bob Cook had said about relating

every event of life to one's commitment, and I had tried to emulate his example. However, I tried to do it as though I were Bob Cook, overlooking at times the grim reality of my being Ken Anderson instead. Unquestionably, we all learn by example. We are admonished in Scripture to be an example.

But I am increasingly convinced the successful Christian goes it alone—with God!

Another mistake lay in thinking the renewing of my mind would be a procedure by which my inferiority complex would vanish, my tendency to self-pity be forever done with, my weaknesses swept under the rug, my cowardice transformed into knighthood!

Wishful thinking.

For God makes no such proposals when He suggests renewal.

During this time, I was assisting Morry Carlson with his Youth Haven project, a year-around camping program for all types of children and youth. We engaged in a test program geared toward rehabilitating boys whose conduct had run askance of the law.

If I had not been a realist before about the foibles of the human species, I quickly became one as, again and again, we witnessed the cruel force of environment upon the mind of a child.

It staggered me.

We had to face up to such unnerving concepts as, "Once a cleptomaniac, always a cleptomaniac," and, in the case of maimed adults, "Once an alcoholic, always an alcoholic."

But doesn't the Bible clearly promise that *"If any man is in Christ, he is a new creature"?* [4]

Yes.

Remember, though, how God assured the apostle Paul, *"My grace is sufficient for thee: for my strength is made perfect in weakness."* [5]

We saw many of those boys at Youth Haven come to

79

Christ, saw change redirect their lives but, through some haunting experiences, we also learned that every one of those chaps entered the Christian experience with his own Achilles' heel.

The lad who had been a thief retained, as his strongest postconversion temptation, the itch of his fingers when he came upon something he wanted.

The lad with a violent temper did not become immune from tantrums.

Those with strong sex impulses did not suddenly become impotent.

I do not for a moment mean to say God cannot bring a total deliverance from prior weakness. I have heard of converted alcoholics, for example, who profess to such dramatic transformation that they have developed a literal loathing for intoxicants. What I do say is that, most commonly, conversion and spiritual growth are spiritual resources which make us master of our weaknesses more often than giving us deliverance from them.

We transcend our hangups rather than getting rid of them.

Note, for example, how Paul adds as his own commentary to God's promise concerning strength and weakness, *"Most gladly therefore will I rather glory in my infirmities, that the power of Christ may rest upon me...for when I am weak, then am I strong."* 6

We are getting to the nub of something tremendous!

The more I consider it, the more convinced I become that a man's total personality is grist for glory.

You do want God to control your life, the Holy Spirit to motivate you, the Bible to serve as a veritable blueprint for activity. Yet do not expect victorious Christianity to be an experience where you are led around by a golden ring in the nose. You sit in the driver's seat instead of being driven. You become the hunter instead of the hunted, the master instead of the slave.

For the very genius of God's method with men is

summarized in the statement, *"Work out your own salvation with fear and trembling. For it is God which worketh in you both to will and to do of his good pleasure."*

Confused?

No need to be.

The situation we face here is the misconception so many Christians have of a victorious life being somehow extra-terrestrial. Saints numbered among the privileged minority sprout wings. They soar above the temptations of life, glide serenely over those troubled waters you so often face, alight for rest only in the sublime heights utterly inaccessible to the likes of us.

It isn't true!

Being a Christian is a human experience. It's the devil's trick to make you think otherwise, to suppose conversion takes you out of this world. Conversion is meant to put you deeper into this world, touching it, conversing with it. That's what witness is all about!

But let's get back to the heart of the matter, you as an earthling and your mind as the seat of existence in the earthly sojourn.

Put it this way: God, incarnate in Jesus Christ, came into this world—a world carnal enough to reject Him—a world cruel enough to crucify Him—a world complacent enough to forget about Him.

But does that immobilize His power and grace?

Not at all.

The world has never been the same since Christ came; it never will be. Every man on earth now has the option of transformation, of rising above the loftiest dream of the philosophers, attaining purity beyond the fondest hope of the moralists.

This is a redeemed world. Men remain under the curse of sin only because they reject the Savior.

Now apply this to your own life.

Jesus Christ has been born in the Bethlehem of your heart.

But you are human, not divine, and you will remain human until you die.

Oh, but doesn't the Bible say, *"If any man is in Christ, he is a new creature; the old things pass away; behold, new things have come"?*

Yes.

This is your state in the grace of God, for becoming a Christian does make a change in your life. Rebirth from lostness into God's family is similar to birth into the physical world. Birth is not maturity, for maturity comes with growth. Those latent virtues which the grace of God brings to you through conversion must be developed in growth just as personality and mentality and physical strength emerge through growth.

As physical growth depends upon gastronomical processes in the stomach, so spiritual growth depends upon *the renewing of your mind.* Through the Holy Spirit, God wants to help you develop a mentality whereby you harness your intellectual and spiritual capacities, causing them to function for His glory and your good.

I'm still searching, and will be as long as I'm bound by mortality, but let me share with you some of the high points I have come upon along what I consider to be the true glory road—namely, the day-by-day relevance of life to the eternal.

I believe the creation of every human being has a dual dimension—the person himself, and the plan God has for this person in the world. What's more, I'm convinced that each of us comes specifically equipped to fulfill that plan, that God's purpose is to be both Architect and Artisan.

I once chafed at my limitations.

I don't anymore.

I'm convinced that—utterly human though I am, at times my own worst enemy—my physical appearance, my mind, my personality, my traits, my talents (and lack of talents!), everything about me is exactly as it should be to fulfill God's plan for my life.

Yours is a similar endowment.

In reality, then, we do not have limitations but abundance!

The same holds for circumstances. What else can be the meaning of Romans 8:28, *"We know that God causes all things to work together for good to those who love God, to those who are called according to his purpose."* [8]

I'm not talking about blind fatalism—such as the Presbyterian who reportedly fell down the stairs, painfully collected himself as he sighed, "Well, thank God, that's over!" I'm talking about events which occur in your life because you have learned to consciously commit the total of it, little things and big things, mountaintops and valleys, in an act of faith to Jesus Christ.

Wally Olson, our business manager, spends his days in a wheelchair. People look at him and feel sorry until they have spent five minutes in his presence. Then they discover one of the most positive men you could meet anywhere. Infectious of spirit, he radiates blessing to everyone in our organization; he is a shining light in our town. He has coached Little League baseball, is the number one rooter for our high school athletic teams, a ruling elder in our church (Presbyterian, incidentally), hasn't an enemy in the world.

Days go by and I don't think of him being in a wheelchair. You just don't see the limitation. You see Wally and the smiling triumph of his Christian faith.

"This wheelchair came into my life at just the right time," he says. "I had my own plans all figured out, but physical adversity was just what I needed to fit me into the plan God has for me."

I've never asked Wally, probably because the answer seems already too obvious, but I'm sure he's human enough to say that, if he had his own personal desires, he would want to be ambulatory. But the moment of birth introduces the process of death. An athlete of thirty is "aging." By forty the gray hairs have begun to appear. Then paunch, skin wrinkles.

We are so obviously transients on this earth. What can it possibly matter then about our material status in comparison to our eternal future? No wonder the Bible asks, *"What does it profit a man to gain the whole world, and forfeit his soul?"* 9

As in the case with your body, so it is with your personality quirks.

I will, of course, cloak them with anonymity, but some of the greatest attestations of the power of God I have witnessed lie in the conduct of people with sharp tongues and quick tempers, people by nature quick to judge others, prone to gossip—but people who not only rise above these faults but, through the power and guidance of the Holy Spirit, reenergize negative traits into positive drives.

For this is what *the renewing of your mind* is all about— it is the Holy Spirit, through the permeation of the Word of God in your frame of reference, making the difference in your attitude, your choices, your motivations.

So much for theological concept.

Now what about the practical side? What are the mechanics of renewal, of transformation?

Going to an altar and signing a decision card can be helpful but surely no more so than starting blocks in a race. *"Grow in the grace and knowledge of our Lord and Savior Jesus Christ,"* 10 the Bible admonishes.

The more I pondered this subject, searched the Scriptures, and prayed, the more I became aware of spiritual process. This is the joy of living, not a static ecstacy but a day-by-day progression of strength built upon strength in glorifying God through our lives.

I began to see the Bible not as a text on doctrine but as a guide to life—abundant life. *"I am come that they might have life,"* Jesus said, *"and that they might have it more abundantly."* 11

Abundance!

Not an abundance of talent, know-how, cleverness, but an abundance of God at work in me, touching my cowardice and giving me courage, touching my weakness and making it strength, placing before the zeroes of my inadequacies the one of omnipotence.

My prayers began to sound something like this: "Lord, show me how to be a better person today than I was yesterday. Shine light upon my faults, so exposing them that I will want to work at changing them with Your help. Inspire me to better human relations, making me a better husband, a better father, an easier person to work with. When I find promises in Your Word, help me apply them to my weaknesses, to depend upon the Holy Spirit to help me get a better stranglehold on those weaknesses. Above all else, God, give me a heart that burns—not with the false glow of mere sentiment but with the kind of fire that builds steam and motivates me to be of some worth to You and be a blessing to people in the rat race of life."

That kind of praying was new to me, and it brought newness to my mind. Little by little, I could see how the Holy Spirit was, in fact, renewing my mind, vitalizing my thought patterns, tempering my reaction time, answering my prayers.

I began to enjoy a concept which has been excitingly dynamic in my life. I call it the initiative factor. Living the Christian life, I discovered, is like playing a game of checkers. When I move, God moves.

And it's always my move!

Now the analogy of a game is limited here. I must move wisely. But when I don't, God chastens me, and I thank Him. For this is part of guidance. But I *can* move wisely, not in my own wisdom but in that wisdom known only to Christians, the wisdom of Christ working in me and making me think and energizing me through the Scriptures and the in-me presence of the Holy Spirit.

The process begins by getting up in the morning and in the first moments of the day acknowledging my relationship to God, my dependence upon Him.

I try to examine my heart for any resistance to His will, any selfish motivations, telling Him that I do in fact want to acknowledge Him in all my ways, to have Him direct my life.

The truth may as well be out here. I'm not the type who rises at four in the morning and spends two hours in Bible study and prayer. I have long admired those who do, and so I do not judge them. Somehow, though I've tried, it doesn't work for me. What does work, however, is to consciously relate every action and every moment of the day to my faith and trust in God. Doing this becomes virtually a subconscious act as, all through the day, I try to depend upon Him to guide me both with restraint and motivation. The test of this procedure comes into closest scrutiny in my relationship to those with whom I live, and through my work.

My wife and I have a deeply meaningful relationship in which we can communicate openly about those faults we see in each other. I find the attitude of my family to be a real test of spiritual growth. The real Ken Anderson is the person my wife and children know.

But for the grace of God, I'd be embarrassed to have you ask them!

This holds with people at work. The organization which I am privileged to lead is by designation evangelical Christian. Unfortunately, I've observed religious organizations similarly classified externally but pockmarked internally with tension and bickering.

You would find little overt spiritual display in our company.

For example, we do not have, as a common practice, extended times of group prayer. I happen to believe, however, that when a company of Christians work together, when they discuss better means of doing their jobs for God's glory, when they brainstorm ideas for more effective spiritual outreach, even when they wrestle with the constant specter

86

of finances, they are actually engaged in the highest form of prayer.

We have a "blue" policy in our company that no matter how effective a film may be which we produce, no matter how widely it is distributed, no matter what the reports may be of spiritual results from the film's screenings, nothing is more important than our attitude, our honesty and openness to each other while we make the film.

To me, this is what the Bible means when it admonishes us to *"work out your own salvation."* [12]

This is how you become a witness to yourself, how the power of God attests in your own life. When that power becomes real to you, when you do become your own best customer, then you have a witness you want to share with others.

The certainty of Christ in your own experience is the strongest apologetic and motivation of the Christian life!

7.
Talking to People Instead of Persons

Just because you observe one fellow Christian witnessing with ease doesn't mean witness comes easy for him. Many Christians, even those who witness regularly, find it their most difficult spiritual function.

Upon boarding a plane for a homeward trip of several hours, I took my assigned seat beside a man reading a newspaper. He glanced at me. I smiled. He smiled in return, then continued reading.

I quietly prayed, asking God to guide me should the opportunity arise for sharing my faith. In the very breath of that prayer, a strong compulsion came over me to talk to him.

But I refrained. It simply isn't my forte to pounce upon a prospect.

I took out a newspaper and began to read. My eyes kept drifting from the page to the man beside me. The compulsion intensified, activating my conscience. I became quite miserable. Was God instructing me to go against my usual procedure of waiting for an opportunity to open?

I noticed that, though he continued reading, the man glanced periodically toward me. I don't intend to be naïvely mystical in such matters, but I have learned that when you ask God for guidance, you can depend upon Him to guide you, and when you are sure of His guidance, obedience becomes imperative.

Just then the man beside me paused from his reading, looked out the window.

"Been a nice day," I said. (Anybody can at least start a conversation by talking about the weather!)

He turned to me, and a warm smile spread across his face.

"Seems like we had a short winter this year," he replied.

Within moments, we got into pleasant conversation, a silent prayer for guidance underscoring my comments and questions. Several times in the exchange between us, I sensed a sure opening for witness, but each time he seemed to deliberately close the door.

Now I know there are those who say I should have come right out with it, given him the sin-suffer-and-repent message followed by a believe-it-or-be-damned ultimatum. But witnessing is relating to persons, not merely pious propaganda to people.

People are faces in a crowd. Persons have feelings. They weep. They laugh. They warm to you or resent you, believe in you or doubt you.

Lord, I breathed in silence, *You laid this man so clearly upon my heart. If You want me to give him Your message, please direct the conversation so I can.*

"What's your line of business?" he asked.

That quickly the opportunity came!

For when men ask me the line of work I'm in, I have a 90 percent opportunity to speak of what Christ has done in my life.

"Our organization produces motion pictures," I said.

"What kind?" he asked.

Right on!

"We primarily supply libraries which rent to churches," I told him.

"Then perhaps I've seen some of your films," he said. "Our church uses motion pictures quite often."

"What church do you attend?"

"One of the Evangelical Free churches in Rockford, Illinois."

He was a believer and, in the next moments, I learned he had been as concerned to talk to me as I had been to talk to him!

"I try to witness when I travel," he said, "but it isn't easy."

"Join the club," I told him.

90

We had several hours of good fellowship, enriching each other's life as we shared experiences.

One doesn't often meet fellow believers, though I have on perhaps a half-dozen other occasions found a traveling companion to be a spiritual compatriot.

Once in Cleveland, while waiting in the airport lobby for a flight connection, a highly personable gentleman came up to me and said, "Pardon me, sir, but I've been watching you for the last twenty minutes. I have a flight to catch. Only got a minute. But my curiosity's got the best of me."

"Do I look like a long-lost relative?" I asked.

"You look to me like someone who knows my Lord," he replied, "someone who is truly Christian."

He caught me completely unprepared!

"Am I right or wrong?" he asked.

"You are right!"

We shook hands.

"I've got to get out to my plane," he excused. "Let's pray for each other, and I'll see you in heaven!"

We didn't even think to exchange names!

How many times has a similar experience been missed because of reluctance on my part to follow the directives of the Holy Spirit!

It is not my purpose to be disobedient, but the pall of timidity hangs perpetually over my head. If there is some secret formula, an *open sesame* to spiritual success, it has escaped my observation.

On the contrary, I have talked to multitudes of Christians, many of them recognized leaders, and the majority speak of personal witness as the most difficult function in the Christian life.

I boarded a plane in the Orient one day and subsequently struck up conversation with the gentleman beside me. Opportunity for witness seemed to loom when he told me he was with the World Health Organization and asked about my occupation.

"I'm in the motion-picture business," I told him, expecting him to express interest and inquire further.

He didn't.

So I added, "We're in the Orient producing a film about the Venture for Victory basketball team."

He remained silent.

"Have you heard of VV?" I asked.

He nodded.

He reached for his briefcase, took out some work, and made it quite obvious he did not care for further conversation.

Quietly, I continued praying.

But no further opportunities came.

After some moments, I strolled to the front of the airplane. Returning, I came upon a man with a large open Bible on his lap. He sat alone.

"Pardon me, sir," I said. "I take it you're a Christian."

"I most certainly am," he replied, looking up pleasantly. "Are you also?"

I nodded, then said, "Your face looks somewhat familiar."

He introduced himself, one of America's outstanding Bible conference speakers, a man whose ministry I had often admired.

"It's good of the Lord to bring us together in this unlikely place," he said. "Tell me about your work."

"First tell me about yours," I said.

He had been invited to several areas in the Orient, conducting Bible conferences for missionaries.

"I find it means a great deal to them," he told me, "having someone from home come to the field and share spiritual blessing. It's a new experience for me. As you know, I speak a good deal in conferences back home but have never done anything like this before and I'm finding it one of the highlight experiences of my entire ministry."

After a few moments, I told him of my curbed conversation with the man from the World Health Organization.

"He seems completely disinterested in the gospel," I said, "and I seem to be very inept at witnessing under such circumstances. Witnessing is quite difficult for me under any circumstances, frankly. Maybe you can give me some advice."

He grew restless.

"How would you go about relating to someone like that?" I asked, anticipating helpful guidance from this seasoned veteran.

"Well," he stammered, "to be quite candid with you, this is probably one of the weakest areas of my life. I find it easy to get up and speak to a very large audience, but I'm afraid I don't have a great deal of success when it comes to the personal encounter."

He seemed so embarrassed at my having brought up the subject I excused myself and slipped back to my seat.

With no intention of taking something from this fine man's ministry, I am forced to assume that—though his ministry is known to Christians throughout Canada and the United States—he is, like me, a coward.

He settled for crowds—for people instead of individual persons.

I share his guilt. I have spoken to service clubs, at graduation commencements, in high school and college convocations, stating my faith with little difficulty. Given the proper set of circumstances, I could with a fair amount of ease have addressed the passengers on that airplane.

But talking to an individual is something else.

"He's got a lot of courage," I've heard it said of some people in Christian work. "When he preaches, he tells it like it is."

So?

During the early years of the Youth for Christ movement, the majority of weekends found me addressing a youth rally somewhere in North America.

My first opportunity came in Grand Rapids, Michigan. Over a thousand had gathered, the largest assembly I had ever faced, and when I got up to speak, my mind went stark blank for an agonizing, endless moment. But I took quickly to rally assignments and graduated to such sites as the Minneapolis Civic Auditorium, Seattle's Moore Theater and Chicago's Orchestra Hall.

A crowd of people can be so very impersonal.

Yet nothing in human experience should be more personal than the transfusion of spiritual life from a living soul to a dead soul. A Christian's highest exploit is to meet an obviously lost person, win his confidence, tell him with tact and optimism that Christ can meet his need.

The Bible says, *"He who is wise wins souls."* [1] Not *"they"* but *"he"*! For in its most effective function, soul-winning is a one-man-to-one-man procedure.

The day came when, in public-speaking assignments, I adopted the procedure of trying to see just one person before me, not simply a sea of faces.

It's not easy.

One-to-one witness, under whatever circumstances, rarely comes as a smooth experience.

I have spoken to missionaries on their field of foreign service who, with tearful eyes, voiced their deepest frustrations. "We have a thrilling ministry in our Bible correspondence courses," one told me, "but I often look out of my office window, see the multitudes going by, and face the frightful fact that months pass without my ever giving personal witness of my faith in Jesus Christ."

Gathering material for this volume, I queried a host of outstanding Christians. Frankly, I was not quite prepared for the results. Anticipating a trove of counsel for the Lord's inept, I discovered instead a host of outstanding Christians facing the same kind of problems you and I face—the compulsion to witness, the willingness, but so often the sense of inadequacy.

Many of us, like the characters in Joseph Bayly's *Gospel Blimp,* look for projects we can help sponsor, missiles we can launch at the enemy while we keep ourselves securely bunkered out of the line of fire.

A prominent Christian author once told me, "Of course, I like to look at myself as a witness through the printed page. To a certain degree I know this is true, and I'm grateful. I have heard of a number of people coming to faith through something I have written, a few of the instances being quite dramatic. But I know the real test of my Christian life lies in faithfulness as a personal witness, and though I try to be alert to this, I readily admit weakness. I don't quite know what to do about it."

Bob Walker, editor of *Christian Life* magazine and protagonist of many spiritual adventures aboard commuter trains as well as on trains and planes while traveling to his numerous editorial responsibilities, told me, "I am probably the best example of blundering witness you can find. Because so many of my contacts are with Christian people, when I do get into a situation where I am with a non-Christian, I fall all over myself trying to get out the witness before it is too late."

He adds, "I'm always impressed when I hear the accounts of those who witness smoothly and with real finesse."

"My problem," confided a prominent Christian businessman, "is that my work is primarily among high-echelon people, with whom religious attitudes are pretty much a private matter. It makes witnessing extremely difficult."

I have addressed church laymen in various parts of the United States, usually gearing my remarks to the problems and procedures of involvement, and as a result have chatted with many different kinds of Christian men. Some were fair-sized titans in business and industry, some outright stalwarts at sales and promotion, but rare is the man who has told me he speaks to others regularly and with ease about his faith.

I particularly remember one man in Des Moines, a big fellow who gripped my hand and said, "It's great to have

95

someone come to our group and share the problems instead of always having someone tell us what we ought to be doing. I expect to sell a million dollars' worth of insurance this year. That's a lot of contact, a lot of talk, and I'll do some witnessing along the way, every chance I can. But I tell you, Ken, it sure is a lot easier talking to a man about life insurance than talking to him about eternal insurance."

Yet I repeatedly meet men who serve as empirical goads to my detested cowardice. Some of them, frankly, leave me a little dubious, like the one who goes about the business of witnessing with the courage of a Kamikaze volunteer, one of his most common moves being to travel from stem to stern of public conveyances thrusting a tract into the hands of each passenger, remaining to drive home the point to any who show interest.

Their number is certainly not legion, these fearless evangelical Quixotes who plunge into situations where angels might hesitate to venture, but they are an awesome lot.

"I like to do house-to-house visitation," one such performer told me. "It's too bad there aren't more Christians willing to do this. It's a natural. You come for a purpose, representing your church, and so you have the opening made for you."

So far I agreed.

But then he said, "I've learned you can't be timid when it comes to telling people about Christ. One of the biggest problems you face calling at home is the television set. You try to talk about the Lord, and you only get half attention. At times, I've just come right out and asked them to turn it off. But that offends some people. So what I often do is move my chair between the people and the TV set. I've had a lot of success with that technique."

We observe a most interesting human trait here.

The best of men have hostility in their hearts. It comes out when we get behind the wheel on the highway. It flares in defense of our offspring when a teacher or a neighbor puts the finger on a child's inadequacies. Regardless of how spiritual we try to be, it taxes our innermost honesty when someone speaks ill of us, particularly if the fault pointed out happens to be true.

The believe-it-or-be-damned approach in witnessing—I speak now of attitude, not of theology—just might in many cases arise from hostility. The witness does not stem from love, from Holy Spirit guidance, but from a compulsion to overpower the benighted and thus give "sanctified vent" to the raw reality of who the soul-winner really is.

Let me go on record here as one who, though reluctant to judge a militant brother, strongly believes tact to be a prime requisite for effective communication.

Granting the existence of those whose tact one might be tempted to question, even those whose performance becomes sufficient reason for nonperformance by other Christians, I meet too many laymen who do witness effectively to permit myself the nonchalance some Christians show to the subject.

One of my most appreciated friendships is with Emerson Ward, successful businessman in our community and nationally prominent member of the Gideons. Though a warmly believable human being, Emerson tends to be the unassuming type, poised and gracious and thoughtful, and most certainly would not strike you as the sort of Christian who stalks the streets adorned by a sandwich board which proclaims *Heaven or Hell—You Must Choose!* on the front and the back.

He isn't that type.

Far from it.

Yet this man annually brings dozens, often scores, of laymen to a place of spiritual decision. He has witnessed to congressmen, governors, Presidents. He represents Christ so uniquely and effectively that one of the prominent wire services carried his exploits to newspapers nationwide a few years ago.

"I try to be sensitive to people's feelings," Emerson says.

97

"Every man has his ego. I know a lot of folks say you should take the static route—tell a man he is a sinner, tell him Christ died for his sins, tell him there is no other way to heaven. All of this is true, of course, and I certainly have no right whatever to criticize those who use that technique. But my approach is to show folks who Jesus is. They're amazed when you show them that Jesus actually created the world and the universe around us, that He is literally God. This means He designed every human being, every one of us. Our bodies are His special craftsmanship. You get a man to really understand who Jesus is, then tell him why Jesus came to the cross, and he'll see his own need of salvation without your having to hammer at him about being lost."

Detroit building tycoon Paul Johnson told me, "I find witnessing comes easiest when you touch a point of common sensitivity. For instance, striking up a conversation, I will mention how unfortunate it is so many men in business have such demanding material goals that they miss the important contributions they should be making to their families, to their kids. I have never met a man yet who didn't agree. When he does, you admit how easily you could get caught in this web yourself if it weren't for the guidance God gives you."

The point is, *witnessing must be personal.* History tells us Constantine had his armies drive men by the thousands to the waters of the Mediterranean for baptism. History also tells us what a fiasco this technique proved to be.

Of course, one hears missionaries speak of the need for group conversion in certain cultures. These are areas where, often due to limited access with the world beyond their immediate habitat, people become enmeshed in a social structure where it becomes virtually impossible for one individual to stand out against the crowd. There are exciting examples of such situations where, by mutual agreement, an entire village has declared itself Christian.

I have attended evangelistic crusades conducted by such

men as Billy Graham, Canada's Barry Moore, the Janz Team in Germany. Night after night I have seen multitudes respond to the quiet, unpressured invitation extended by these men.

Yet, whether it is a village in New Guinea or a crowd in some city of the Western world, conversion only occurs when individuals recognize their need for a personal Savior.

The best of evangelists will readily admit that, however effective a mass meeting may be, nothing supersedes the impact of one man relating his faith to another man.

Person to person! This is where the spark of reality most readily touches tinder.

Please do not permit yourself to be so swept up in theory that you get the impression that witness is completely mystical, that the Holy Spirit does everything as though you were a puppet.

Hardly!

You need to become familiar with the Scriptures. Memorization is most helpful. Campus Crusades' *Four Spiritual Laws* smooth the way for many. A plan which works for you in witness can be helpful.

One of my most cherished acquaintanceships is with Stanley Tam, one of America's unique Christian businessmen and a master at eyeball-to-eyeball evangelism.

"I am driven to insist that every Christian can serve God as a personal soul-winner," Stan says, "because He uses me in this capacity. As a boy, I was afraid of my own shadow. I would go out of my way to avoid meeting people. When newly converted, and the thought occurred to me that I should tell others of my faith, I shrank at the prospect."

Driven by the compulsion to relate his faith to the non-churched, but devoid of courage, Stan bought a 16 mm. movie projector and took evangelistic films to people's homes.

"I would let the film do the preaching," he says, "and the first few times, that was about it. Little by little, though, my confidence grew, and I could relate my faith as well.

Before long, I was able to invite men to Christ. My life has never been the same since!"

Soul-winning is hardly an endeavor calling for scoreboards and the declaration of a national champion, but I personally know of no other layman in America who each year brings more people to the Christian faith than does Stanley Tam. Nor anyone who is more considerate of the needs and feelings of those to whom he witnesses.

How can you and I acquire this adeptness?

I previously mentioned Paul Johnson.

Now I admit Paul is a very likable person. However, he tends to be reserved, certainly not the type who moves into a situation with flailing arms.

But he does witness consistently.

"It is something you learn to do by doing," he told me. "Each time you talk to someone about the Christian life, you become more at ease. You learn by experience. You profit by your mistakes and build upon the strong points you discover."

Can you and I cause the effectiveness of Christians like Stanley Tam and Paul Johnson to rub off onto our own experience? Or must each of us settle for being just another of the "also rans"? Survey indicates no more than 2 percent of the allegedly committed Christians in America make any consistent effort to audibly share their faith.

We know God has no voice but ours. We've gone to the altar, tossed sticks onto summer campfires, prayed for forgiveness, vowed to do better. Yet we realize that if God treated us the way any solvent corporation must react to ineffective salesmen, we would probably be walking the streets.

Remember what we have thus far discovered. You are not Stanley Tam nor Paul Johnson nor—thank God!—the silver-tongued Bible-conference circuit-rider I met on the plane.

You are you!

God has a program for your life, and it consists of working in you, through you. Rest, and at the same time energize, in the search to know all that implies.

Then see people as God sees them. Multitudes of persons who, like you, display all kinds of outward veneer but who, inside, are full of need. Do not approach these persons as a conqueror but as one who stops along life's way to help a fellow traveler.

Be person to person in all of life's relationships and you will by impulse become personal in your witness!

Witnessing is not some kind
of sport in which you
endeavor to bag a daily
   GAME LIMIT...

8.
Experts at Following Orders!

Your success as a Christian doesn't depend on you—your cleverness or lack of talent—but on your willingness to accept and activate God's pledge to guide you in every responsibility and relationship.

"I'm convinced one of our problems in witnessing is that we talk too much," Don Lundeen, one of my close associates in business, says. "If we will be open and friendly to people, but give them more of our ear and less of our tongue, we can determine their thinking, their concerns, their fears. Then we can do a lot better job telling them about our faith."

Paul Van Oss, executive director of YFCI, says, "For years, I struggled to live the Christian life. Most of the time my struggles brought me only defeat and failure. Then, desperate, I asked the Lord to take over my life and to live His life through me. Now, by His help, I invest each moment in a conscious attempt to allow the risen Lord freedom to move in and through me in a power that makes my Christian life a whole new experience."

Russ Reid, Los Angeles advertising consultant, told me, "I'm fortunate in that it has never been difficult for me to talk to people about any subject. So, by some Christian's definition, witnessing comes easy for me. There was a time in my life when I'd get into a taxi and bluntly ask the driver if he knew Jesus Christ as his personal Savior. It seemed a very simple procedure to manipulate this person into a commitment. But I've come to wonder if this isn't ego manifesting itself and not witness at all. I'm not timid, have no difficulty relating to people, but I'm increasingly sensitive to the fact that I must not intrude on someone else's religious convictions until I'm sure God has prepared the way for me to share my faith."

I get a touch of nostalgic fright when I hear my friends talk this way, because it reminds me how long I blundered in the Christian life before it occurred to me what the apostle Paul was saying when he wrote *"Christ in you"*[1] and *"it is God who is at work in you, both to will and to work for His good pleasure."* [2]

I find myself easily skeptical of some people who give profuse accounts of receiving inner-voice directions, of opening the Bible and putting down a finger and thereby obtaining specific instructions. I do recognize, of course, the mystical aspects of the Christian life, and that we are human and in communion with the Divine.

We produced a film on the life of Sadhu Sundar Singh, the incredible Indian Christian. In researching the story, we found a trove of amazing anecdotes, situations where this man seemed to be in outright voice-to-voice communion with the Lord. Some of these instances, while I would hesitate to discredit them, were so unusual we felt they could not be scripted for fear pragmatic Westerners would shrug off the entire story as fiction.

Missionaries will tell you, however, that voices and visions are not uncommon in the conversion and growth of many Orientals.

I've seen no visions, heard no ethereal voices, but I do believe in guidance. God says, *"I will guide thee with mine eye,"* [3] and I believe He means it. What's more, I believe my Christian life will wash out without that guidance.

Here's a simple little policy helpful to me on this point: Learn the principles of the Christian life as spelled out in the Scriptures. Recognize your own frailty, your ego, your limitations. Then invite the Holy Spirit to direct you within the context of Scripture.

He will!

A very helpful rule is to let actions speak much more

articulately than words. True spirituality is less argumentative than demonstrative. A Christian should never be more gracious than when he is affronted, when he disagrees.

It's summed up in the word *love*!

Love is the ether wave of the spiritual world—a context in which God, through the Holy Spirit, guides you and makes valid your response in relation to others.

One of the reasons laymen have so many opportunities for Christ's cause these days is that worldlings are looking for spiritual answers right where they are, in the sweat and smudge of life as they know it; and when they see someone relating faith to that kind of life, it registers.

But God must show us how to adequately relate our faith. To accomplish this, I'm convinced that, even as He has equipped us individually to do His will, so He has fashioned the world as a place where His children can effectively witness.

For example, we know there are unseen forces in our world which constantly affect human conduct and relationships. We call these psychological, invisible dynamics, the winds and tides and currents of mortal persuasion. I believe each valid psychological force in this world is a divinely ordained law—as much as gravity, energy and inertia are laws of the physical world.

God did not place in motion the high-psychological octane which fuels Madison Avenue advertising machinery in order that Schlitz could sell more beer and General Motors more automobiles. The laws which undergird good organization, effective salesmanship and productive human relations have as their primordial purpose the enablement of you and me to articulate God's grace to a lost world.

Some people apply these laws as naturally as they breathe, resulting in that distinct charisma possessed by the fortunate few. They bypass the hangups we introverts must live with.

I envy such people. I can't help it.

However, I think it's often a lot harder for superbly talented folk to live the Christian life than it is for us cowards. A man who has orbiting confidence in himself, who influences people and gets the things he wants with minimum effort, must be on constant guard against overconfidence.

But people like us—those who must constantly face up to their limitations—are prime candidates for God's special strength and wisdom. We need power beyond ourselves, and we know it.

Among the many lessons learned during my China experience was how relatively unimportant human attributes can be in the successful outreach to others.

I spent a week in Nanchang with China's outstanding evangelist, Andrew Gih. We were met at the train station by a tall, gangly man named Robert Porteus. I stood at the brink of the other side of the generation gap in those days, and this somewhat uncomely individual struck me very negatively with his effusive manner.

"You'll be spending the week in our home!" he exclaimed.

Just my luck, I bemoaned.

When he showed me to my room, I noted the absence of security for valued possessions, or any way to lock my door.

"My camera was stolen out of my room while I slept in Tsingtao," I quipped. "Missionaries in every place have warned us to keep valuables out of sight from servants."

"You'll have no trouble here," he said. "The Lord has graciously permitted us to lead our workers to the Savior and they love His Word and seek to honor Him. Everything is safe in your room."

Long before the week was out, I asked God's forgiveness for the way I had prejudged this marvelous man. He lacked charisma but he radiated Christ. The last time I saw him, he was in his eighties and running a servicemen's center. The GI's loved him!

A perfect combination of forces, then, stands at your disposal as you endeavor to serve God. From Him come wisdom, love, patience, tact. Surrounding those you seek to touch are the psychological laws of persuasion, confidence, motivation.

Through you divine laws and human principle mesh.

Precisely how, though, do we let God make us convincingly usable?

The more I struggled with that question, the more I searched the Bible for answers, the more I honestly appraised myself and assessed my goals, the more two words loomed distinct in my thoughts.

Obedience.

Guidance.

Here we need a careful preface.

While I believe the Christian life should be a serious and all-consuming venture, I reject the pietistic approach on the simple grounds of this being the day of the materialist.

Since childhood, I've sat under the ministry of many pastors. Some seemed to cloister themselves away in towers of ecclesiastical mien or scholarship. A few—altogether too few—truly bridged the space between the sacred page and the secular world.

But there have been refreshing exceptions.

One such was Pastor Dick.

A most unique man of the cloth, he doubled as chaplain of the police force in our town, riding with squad cars on calls, because he knew the action was most often found where men use four-letter words other than "Lord," "pray" and "save."

Pastor Dick helped me look for exuberance in Christian living. "If we can't have fun serving God," he said, "I believe something's wrong with us. Living the Christian life is mighty serious business. Whatever we do for a living, Christianity must be our vocation, not merely an avocation. But if we live our faith as God intended, we live a life of joy."

That kind of grass-roots theology proved disturbing to

some in our community. It made a lot of sense to me, though. I've become strongly suspect of Christians who painstakingly engineer themselves into being pious. Becoming burdened for a lost world doesn't involve assuming the countenance of a prude; instead, it consists of honest, observable demonstration of God's ability to lift a man above the pressures and uncertainties of life with *songs in the night*,[4] however dark the darkness.

This kind of Christianity isn't something a man drums up, however. It's something he permits God to lead him into. For you can't find the way yourself, no matter how resourceful you may be. And those of us with lesser talent endowments are as much candidates for this guidance as Christians supercharged with natural ability.

The mark of spirituality, you know, is not being drawn farther away from the full life into an aesthetic chrysalis. Rather, the truly spiritual man is one who becomes increasingly believable as a human being, following the pattern of Jesus who *"kept increasing in wisdom and stature, and in favor with God and man."* [5]

I tend to become a bit overt on this point because of the fortifications in my own experience.

A result of my writing career was a part-time editorial position with what is now *Campus Life* magazine, and through this I came into close association with such influential leaders of youth evangelism as Torrey Johnson, Cliff Barrows, T.W. Wilson, Billy Graham and Chuck Templeton.

I was completely awed by these men.

At that time, only Torrey Johnson had vaulted into prominence as a national figure, but the others possessed those aptitudes which were to guide them in the several directions of renown.

Most notable today, of course, is Billy Graham. I frequently ghosted magazine articles for Billy. He was cooperative and appreciative, often remarking about the strength I had given to some of his concepts. I was grateful for his commendation, but also troubled. If I could speak with authority through the keys of a typewriter, why couldn't I be just as lucid with my tongue?

About this time I became involved with some other youth leaders in a study program designed to help teenagers come to grips with spiritual commitment. The more I researched my phase of this responsibility, the more I thought about it, the closer I drew to a wonderful discovery.

Those of us involved in the project were asked to do some thinking on procedures whereby young people could harness the reality of themselves, relating that reality to the potentials of their faith.

I sat in my study one night, doodling as I often do when trying to ferret out ideas, and took a piece of paper and drew a line down the center. At the top of the page, on the left-hand side, I wrote, *Strength and Talents*. On the right-hand side, I wrote, *Faults and Weaknesses*.

Nonchalantly at first, I jotted a few items on the left side, then a few on the right. Suddenly the importance of what I was doing began to dawn on me!

Remember my saying that we cowards can learn to make our inadequacies work for us instead of against us? That's precisely what this little exercise did for me.

Humility, you know, is a synonym for honesty. As I became honest about my faults and weaknesses, I felt encouraged to be equally honest about my strengths and abilities, and I was not only amazed to find how many positives I could enumerate but, in comparing the two columns, to see how many of my strengths were applicable therapy for many of the weaknesses.

For example, one of my weaknesses is that I am quite nongregarious. I doubt if I could become a hermit, but I much prefer being alone with a good book or my typewriter or a film to cut than hobnobbing with a crowd. I am, frankly, what you might call a people-hater, with a special disdain for giddy women.

On the left-hand side of the page, however, under *Strengths and Talents*, I had listed, "I enjoy showing courtesy and kindness to others."

Which is true.

Once I get to know someone, or become involved in a cause or presentation, I'm an exceedingly soft touch. My wife is a woman of poise and generosity, but she is also astute, and she has many times spared me the after-misery of contributing the shirt off my shoulders to some enterprise of dubious qualification.

A cry of praise rose to my heart in that moment. Could I not here interrelate strength and weakness to the enrichment of my life? I could and, thank God, I have!

My God has given me a new love and appreciation for people. It's His doing, not mine, because my old Adamic often crops up, making it necessary for me to pray, "Lord, let Your love flow through my life," and God always answers that prayer!

I am discovering what Paul talked about when he told the Christians at Rome that their bodies should not be *"conformed to this world,"* but *"transformed by the renewing of your mind."* 6

I began applying this simple spiritual exercise to other areas of the strength-and-weakness pattern, with highly satisfactory results. Let me be quick to underscore, however, that the vitality of this procedure had as its inner force a new application of prayer.

Prayer and praise.

When weakness rears its ugly brow in my experience, I simply ask God to help me apply the strength with which He has endowed me to counteract this weakness, and invariably He does. And when He does, I praise Him for it. Gratitude is the master key to many doors.

This practice led me to the place where I sought to maintain perpetual communion with God throughout the day, thanking Him for blessings, asking Him for guidance. And it was here, in the request for guidance, that I found at last the road map to successful witness!

Oh, I'm sure if I became absolutely convinced God wanted me to barge into the house of some unredeemed man and begin telling him of his need for salvation, I'd do it. It would, however, be completely foreign to my personality, and the longer I walk with God, the more I'm convinced He made me the way He did so I could serve Him in a manner harmonious with my traits and talents.

As you can surmise, I do very little barging.

I believe there is a much better way.

Paul challenged the Thessalonians to *"pray without ceasing."* 7 That doesn't mean to get into a closet and onto our knees and pray all day when we ought to be out in the marketplace serving as epistles *"known and read of all men."* 8

My procedure is to go through the day in a normal pattern, consciously relating the actions and the decisions of the day to my confidence in God. If a salesman comes into my office, if I'm with an uncommitted acquaintance, if I board a plane, wherever I may be in the presence of people with potential need, I habitually pray, *Lord, here I am, one of Your children. You know how weak and timid I am. You know how easy it is for me just to keep quiet. But if You open the door for me to bear witness of Your grace to this person, I'll do it, by Your help.*

I'm convinced God takes special delight in answering such a prayer!

You see, successful witness is not you doing the work. It's you used of the Holy Spirit, letting Him work through you.

Witnessing is not some kind of sport in which you endeavor to bag a daily game limit. Witnessing is being God's workman, in league with Him. You wouldn't jar the arm of a surgeon during a delicate operation. Neither should you jar God's hand. He knows what He's doing. He knows whom He wants you to influence. And if you will ask Him,

111

keeping your mind and heart continually sensitive to His guidance, if you will be obedient to that guidance, He will show you.

The easiest thing for me when I board an airplane is to open my briefcase and select a file for work. But my first routine is to remind God of my availability to serve Him if the Holy Spirit unlatches the door to opportunity. If someone sits beside me, I smile. Sometimes that's as far as it goes. Often, however, the smile leads to conversation. Sometimes conversation is as far as it goes. Again and again, however, conversation leads to an opening where, by applying tactful initiative, I steer a casual parlance into an opportunity to witness.

I never cease to be amazed at how feasible witness becomes when I go at it on the basis of following God's orders!

Does this mean I've rubbed out the yellow streak down my back?

No.

But I am learning to apply God's promises to me. The apostle John says, *"This is the confidence which we have before Him, that, if we ask anything according to His will, He hears us."* [9]

His will is for me to be victorious, not defeated, as a Christian. When cowardice rears its ugly head in my life, His will is for me to experience the Holy Spirit's infinite capacity to make faith the antidote for knee-quaking mortality. When I cringe at facing up to a difficult encounter or decision, His will is for me to demonstrate the special poise and glow only a Christian can experience, because only a Christian has the built-in capacity to serve as a conductor—not the generator!—of divine light and power.

That's what transformation is all about!

It isn't easy for me to witness to someone. I suppose it never will be. I like the way Bill Pearce puts it: "Isn't it almost always this way?" he asks. "Men of God in past ages, and even many today, may not have had the natural ability to communicate their faith. Instead, in fear and trembling, they've allowed the Holy Spirit to witness through them!"

That's it!

Obedience!

No one can prescribe or predict how obedience will activate your witness patterns. The God who allows no two snowflakes to share a common design wants to give freshness and spontaneity to each Christian's experience. There is unity in the fellowship of the committed, of course, but there should never be an establishment, no party line, no pat set of rules.

In Toledo, Sam and Marilyn Bender use their fine capacity at hosting to relate their faith to members of the country club set. Sam, a young industrialist, met Marilyn during a United Airlines flight out of Chicago. There was rough air, and Marilyn, a stewardess, spilled coffee on Sam's sleeve. They married, were subsequently converted, and members of the evangelical community urged them to immediately break ties with the cocktail crowd.

They didn't.

It became part of their transformation to give up the cocktails, but a goodly number of social registerites thank God the Benders listened to Him instead of their well-intentioned consultants.

My good friends, the Cooles, live in a London suburb. He's a medical doctor. Wife Priscilla has a superb knack for making guests feel at ease. Their house and garden, in fine English decor, have become a special sanctuary to many.

In a nation where something like 2 percent of the populace can be found in church on a given Sunday, Dr. Coole says, "Sunday is the only free day many professional people have and, unfortunately, the church no longer attracts them. We find social relationships to be a wonderful opportunity, however. We go to the cocktail parties, though neither of us imbibes. Then we invite our friends to our house, and they have never evidenced the slightest indication of being affronted by the fact we do not serve liquor."

"Winning such people is a slow process," Priscilla adds. "We usually invite small groups, as this gives better opportunity for witness. These people long for sincere friendship. They feel estranged from the world, even from their children. They have everything money can offer, and yet they have nothing."

It's a slow process for the Cooles, but they now have a Bible class in their home regularly attended by twelve converts!

Waddy Spoelstra, who follows the Tigers for the Detroit *News*, champions the cause of the ballplayer who's having a rough go of it. He'll turn a complimentary paragraph for a sagging hitter who happens to have a good day. Waddy's genuineness opens the door for witness to many in the sports world.

Nigel Cooke operates a chain of coin laundries in Britain, teams with wife Helen in a special ministry for young couples.

Keith Rowe is an architect in Trinidad, uses his drawing board as a springboard for witness.

Ray Carlson, as an American engineer building an ultramodern refinery for an oil cooperative in Sweden, joined wife Joy, with assists from their two fine children, in heralding a compelling spiritual example for many Swedes shortchanged by their complacent progenitors.

Ray Clendenan, the amazing get-the-job-done Michigan farmer, serves as special consultant to the dairy industry, to the U.S. Department of Agriculture, and finds time to spearhead a growing Youth for Christ program in the Thumb area.

Harry Elders is a Chicago actor whose biggest concern is not for lucrative residuals from radio and television commercials but opportunities to talk about Christ to people in the business.

For our daughter Margaret, following God's guidance is to teach in a community riven with racial tensions. We live for the weekends when Marg returns to tell us of new opportunities she's had to witness to her students. "You're soul, Miss Anderson!" black girls tell her.

God has a spot for you to fill too. A big spot—because it encompasses the full dimensions of His plan for your life! You can find that spot, find it and fill it, only as you seek God's guidance and obey His directives. Only as you let Him do His work in you.

I like the way Bill Garthwaite, one of our film distributors, puts it: "Somehow the average Christian seems to feel that bearing fruit involves a go-go-go situation. So few understand that it is *yet not I, but Christ living in me.*"

9.
Chapter and Verse

Though you don't use the Bible like a celestial tommy gun, you do need it as the prime basis for your witness.

Christians unfamiliar with the Bible, and particularly those who have never committed strategic areas to memory, are like a hunter who buys an expensive gun, sets out in search of game, then realizes he neglected to purchase ammunition.

I owe much to the Sunday school I attended as a boy. Teachers used the International Sunday School Lessons and, at closing exercises, each of us was given a chance to recite the golden text, or some other passage we might have memorized. One girl, Sunday after Sunday, settled for *"Draw nigh to God, and he will draw nigh to you'* [1] for as long as I could remember. But I learned the golden text every week, adding to the store in later years, and this programming of spiritual data has been of intrinsic value to me.

Don't think of the Bible as some kind of gimmick, however. The Word of God is a resource for comfort and guidance, not a weapon with which to fell the wayward. If you could corner every person in the world and quote John 3:16 to him in his own language, you would not thereby have the world evangelized. You might conceivably have done more harm for the cause than good.

I heard one man say, "When you witness to a sinner, Brother, put the Bible on him and watch him cringe."

That technique may be well intentioned, and in some instances better than no witness at all, but I'm dubious.

In the years since World War II, the American home has

117

been deluged with new translations and paraphrases of the Scriptures. This has been a boon to Bible study, with so many scholarly shades of meaning to compare in digesting a portion of Scripture.

But which version do you memorize?

You doubtless heard of the well-meaning chap who proclaimed, "I'm sticking with the King James Version. If it was good enough for the apostle Paul, it's good enough for me!"

The New American Standard Bible, produced by the Lockman Foundation, is a faithful translation from the original languages and is excellent. I personally recommend it for memorization, using other modern English treatises for Bible study.

But the point is—memorize!

How can you expect the Holy Spirit to lead you in witness if you do not know what verses from the Bible to use in counseling one who seeks to know Christ?

A word of caution here.

Back to the chap who said, "Put the Bible on him and watch him cringe," I'm not so sure this is the best technique. For in this instance, the zealot boasted of being able to reel off verse after verse from the tip of his tongue.

That could be an exercise of the ego.

I've found it helpful to know where a verse is in the Bible, but to turn to it as one does in normal Bible study, and then share it with the seeker. I've even said, "Pardon me while I check the concordance a moment" as I've counseled someone in my study.

One thing is sure: the Bible must be central to soul-winning. For you can never philosophize a sinner into the kingdom.

Be sure you have confidence in the Bible. If you don't have confidence, ask God for it. *"Examine everything carefully,"* the Bible tells you. *"Hold fast to that which is good."* [2] This includes the Bible. You don't take it blindly at face value; you take it at faith value!

On the other hand, all this dispute today about whether the Bible is or isn't the authoritative Word of God would amuse me if it weren't so tragic. I see as much sense in arguing with my wife as to whether or not the corn flakes topped with blueberries which she served me for breakfast were food. I know that was food because I ate it and it satisfied me and gave me energy for this morning's work!

And in witness I'm more convinced that it's what the Bible has done for me that counts, not simply what it can do for the person to whom I witness. When I can tell someone about the coming of poise and relevance to my life, about the way God has so adequately met the needs of our children as they've struggled with the biological and intellectual and social issues in their lives, this is of far greater initial importance than simply quoting Bible verses.

Ray Clendenan says, "I rarely use Scripture when giving my witness. I've seen people become offended when you try to push the Bible at them. But when someone expresses interest in receiving the Christian faith for himself, that's another matter. Then it's absolutely necessary to be able to give applicable Bible verses to substantiate what you've told them Christ has done for you and can do for them."

Whether or not you quote the Bible when you witness, your witness must be biblically accurate. The Bible is a book of transforming concepts and motivating ideas, and your commission is to get these ideas and concepts across to those whom the Holy Spirit brings alongside your path.

My study is actually a shack in back of our house, and it has become a special sanctuary at times when the Holy Spirit has permitted me to share my faith with others. One such case was one of the most outstanding young athletes ever to come out of our town. (We live in Indiana, where basketball is known as Hoosier Hysteria.)

"I just can't believe anything," he told me. "I'm not even sure there's a supreme Being."

Reading Scripture brought a blank stare to his eyes. I

119

later learned a relative had previously "put the Bible on him and watched him cringe."

I gave him a copy of Dr. Francis Schaeffer's *Escape from Reason*, told him of my own research into the philosophies of men.

Some would condemn me for this approach.

But perhaps you've heard of the prime rule in witness that we "must earn the right to be heard." I strongly subscribe to that rule. Rush into a thinking pagan's office, tell him, "Mister, if you don't believe in Christ and turn from your sins, you'll go to hell," then quote chapter and verse, and you'll likely drive him farther from faith than closer to it.

I logged many hours with a young man whose faith was shipwrecked when, in the Sunday school of a fundamental church, the teacher of a class of boys shook his finger in this kid's face and thundered, "You should get down on your knees and ask God's forgiveness for asking those kind of questions about the Bible!"

In talking to such young people, I've found it helpful to say something like this: "Look, so you have hangups about the Bible? I have some myself. Many things I don't understand. But I *do* know the Bible has met my need, and the needs of multitudes. Approach it this way: You aren't sure. You question. OK? But can you settle for this definition, that 'In whatever manner God intended it to be, the Bible is His inspired Word'?" Again and again, this has broken the ice and opened an opportunity to then share the Scriptures.

The father of one young man called me at my office and said, "I don't know what you're doing for my boy, but he says he's sure Mr. Anderson has the right religion."

One of those fellows wrote to me from college. He said, "I sure do appreciate all the things you told me, and it's helped a lot to get some things straight in my mind. I know I have a long way to go yet, but one wonderful thing has happened to me. In thinking over those things you told me, I now believe there is a God. It's a wonderful feeling because, when I was in high school, I lost complete confidence in God altogether."

Few people realize we are living in the post-Christian era of the Western world. Young minds are not conditioned toward faith, as was once the case, but against it. This is the time when intellectuals speak of absurdity and despair as the only realities.

But God can help us to help such young people find faith through the Bible!

I met a chap once who said, "I can just feel the strength of Scripture when I hold the Bible in my hands."

Nonsense!

In its material form of pages and print, the Bible has no more power or authority than a telephone book. Only when I read it, when I permit its living concepts to permeate my frame of reference, only then does the Bible function with power in my life.

Now please don't charge me with heresy when I say I'm not sure the actual quotation of the Bible is in every case necessary to convey spiritual truth. I do quote my Bible when I witness. I do endeavor to stay close to its verbatim message. But just as important as quoting, *"The righteous man shall live by faith,"* 3 is, in my opinion, to put into the words of my own experience a contemporary recounting of how my faith in God adds up in specific needs I face as a human being.

In other words, don't be as concerned about showing someone in need how the Bible reads in print as you are concerned to show him how it adds up when applied to the stress and strain of life itself.

And by all means, try always to avoid embarrassing the person to whom you talk. I've watched Christians, toting a Bible the size of a Sears Roebuck catalog, plunk it in front of an unsuspecting prospect. The poor fellow squirmed, not because of deep conviction, as the would-be harvester believed, but because he wasn't accustomed to appearing in public places with an emblem of such pronounced piosity.

On the other hand, times will come when you need to use the Scriptures—I recommend a small New Testament or one of the new versions in normal book binding—and the one to whom you relate will find it helpful to read for himself what God has to say about emergence from doubt and darkness into faith. At such times, I know of no substitute for a working knowledge of what the Bible says and where it says it.

For instance, I got into conversation with a university student who listened attentively to my witness, then suddenly blurted, "OK, what can you do for a guy like me? I have absolutely no faith!"

He caught me off guard. Not so off guard, however, as to prevent me from breathing a silent prayer reminding God of His promise that *"if any of you lack wisdom, let him ask."*[4]

"Take a good look at me," I said, surprised at my own words, "because I don't have any faith either."

His eyes widened with suspicion. "You're putting me on," he said.

"It's the truth."

"But you've been telling me about your faith."

"Oh, I live by faith; it's the mainstream of my life. But this faith isn't something I've generated myself. It's something which has come to me from an outside source. You can go to the same source for faith as I do. Interested?"

"I sure am."

I opened my New Testament and let him read Romans 10:17, *"Faith comes from hearing, and hearing by the word of Christ."*[5]

Within the hour, I had the privilege of assisting him make his profession of faith.

On a recent trans-Atlantic flight, I sat beside a member of the Swedish Trade Commission. He was reading Dag

Hammarskjöld's *Markings*, a book I had perused with much profit, and after a quiet prayer for guidance, I felt inclined to comment on the book.

He was pleased.

Soon we were talking about Hammarskjöld's faith, a rarity among Swedes these days.

I was heading homeward from a film assignment with the Christian Council of Kenya, which prompted my new acquaintance to ask, "Have you had opportunity to become personally aquainted with Africans?"

"Many of them," I replied.

"What is your opinion of African culture?"

"It intrigues me. I had a lot of the preconceived notions about cannibals and people with rings in their noses. There has been this aspect of Africa, of course. But what completely surprises me is to discover the dignity of the African. Even in remote villages, where life goes on as it has for many generations, the African has a dignity seldom seen in the so-called civilized world. I was also impressed with the African's basic cleanliness."

"Then what's the point of disturbing the African's culture with religious ideas from the white race? We can't learn to live at peace with ourselves. What right have we to try to indoctrinate others?"

I could have said something about my opinions of Swedish neutrality. (Incidentally, all four of my grandparents were born in Sweden.) Instead, I told him about the universality of man's need, that I don't think there is such a thing as a Christian nation, that men everywhere need to find God in a personal, comprehensible relationship.

Then I told him of several of my new Christian Masai friends—like John Impai, who heads the Bible Society in Kenya; like Daniel Sindayo who was then chief warden of the famed Amboselli Game Reserve—men whose discovery and implementation of the Christian faith have built, in less than a lifetime, a bridge five hundred years long between them and their immediate forebears.

I told him of the peace and purpose in my own life. We discussed our families, the war in Vietnam, and I shared with him the testimony of our soldier son, Lane, stationed at that time in Long Binh, twenty-five miles from Saigon.

"Your faith is exciting to you," he said. "That isn't the usual thing."

"I'm afraid I disagree," I said. "Anyone who experiences genuine Christian faith usually finds it exciting."

In spite of his reserved attitude, there was no hiding now his extreme interest in what we were talking about. I prayed for guidance. Here was a man of high intellect, of obvious prejudices, and of little if any spiritual background.

In my briefcase, I had a copy of *Living Gospels* which I took out and showed to him. He had never seen anything like this before, the Bible in contemporary diction. As I've done previously in such encounters, I offered the book to him as a gift.

He refused, politely at first, staunchly when I became more insistent. But he did take the publisher's address and promised to secure a copy as soon as he reached New York, where he would be living for the next year.

In this case, I sensed no opportunity to quote Scripture, so I didn't. Nor could I discern any evidence of this man being ready to make commitment. I'm convinced the Holy Spirit's purpose was for me to introduce a highly sophisticated individual to the Word of God.

I endeavor to guide such a person into the gospel of John. For if you find someone who honestly looks for spiritual enlightenment, and if you can get this person to read the gospel of John, you've taken a long stride toward helping him meet his Savior.

I came across a chap in Wisconsin who directed a rock-and-roll combo. His mother, unfortunately, was one of those hard-at-it Evangelicals, woefully short on tact.

He wore a purple sport coat and gold trousers. As we talked, he kept snapping his fingers and tapping his left foot. Rhythm was obviously his thing.

"My ma's got me unsold on religion," he said.

"I'm not very sold on religion myself," I countered, "but I'm interested in getting everything I can out of life. That's what faith's all about, to help us get the most out of living."

This caught his interest.

"Let me ask you something," I said. "Don't you sometimes get up in the morning, after you've had a big night, and take a look at yourself in the mirror and wonder if you might be cheating yourself?"

"Yeah—" he mumbled. "Yeah—I do that sometimes."

All the time I spoke to him, I was silently praying. Prayer must always undergird our times of sharing.

"If you thought God had something for you that you really can't afford to miss, would you be interested in finding it?" I asked.

"If God's got something like that, it's a cinch my ma hasn't found it."

"Let's talk about you, OK?"

"OK."

"Do you have a Bible?"

He grinned. "Do I have a Bible? Ma gives me one every Christmas!"

"Ever read the Bible?"

"Been a long time."

"Do you know where the gospel of John is?"

"Sure. Matthew, Mark, Luke, John."

"Look," I said, "I dare you to read the gospel of John. As you read, tell God that if He's got something you want and are missing, you're open to receive it. Would you do that?"

"I just might.˙

A couple of years passed. In the hustle of other things, I forgot about this chap. Then I was asked to speak at a laymen's night observance in a church in the area. At the close, a young couple came to me. The man was well groomed, dressed in fine taste. The girl held his arm in such a manner as to prominently display her engagement ring.

"Remember me?" the young man asked.

I looked at him a moment, drew a blank.

"You're sure you don't remember me?"

"Afraid not," I said, somewhat embarrassed. "Sorry."

He began snapping his fingers rhythmically and tapping his left toe, grinning at me.

Then I remembered!

"Man, how that Bible grabbed hold of me!" he exclaimed. "You got my curiosity up, and so I did read the gospel of John. I prayed, like you said. When I got about two-thirds through, it all of a sudden got through to me that I was buying what I read. I started believing in Jesus, right while I read about Him in the Bible!"

He introduced me to his fiancé, a Christian girl he met following his conversion, and told me of their impending nuptials and their determination to establish a Christian home.

Now, in fullest honesty, I want to admit to a problem I have. I say "problem" because it would be so classified by many of my friends.

"When you witness," I've so often been told, "it's important to properly represent the product, but you've also got to ask for a sale." Frankly, getting the "sale" doesn't come easy for me.

Concerning evangelism, Paul wrote to his Christian brothers at Corinth, *"I planted, Apollos watered, but God was causing the growth."* 6

Mine seems to be more the ministry of planting and watering than of harvest.

In one community where we lived, an outstanding civic leader and his wife became friends of ours and, as a result, we had hours of opportunity to share our faith with them. They were cut right out of the mold of twentieth-century unbelief, had absolutely no confidence in the Bible, doubted conversion as anything but a psychological phenomenon, even questioned the existence of God.

126

How we longed to bring them to Christ!

We didn't but, several years later, we learned one of them had become a Christian and the other was near to decision. Really, now, my wife and I rejoiced just as much in this as if we had brought the decision ourselves by God's help.

I think God gives a special gift of harvest to some people.

Billy Graham declares he cannot understand how, after simple gospel messages and a brief, quiet invitation, thousands come forward to make public proclamation of faith. "It is a gift from God," he says. "I would be powerless if God ever took His hand off of me."

This is why obedience and guidance are so important.

Initiative?

To be sure.

But let it always be initiative prompted by the Holy Spirit. He alone can draw men to Christ.

When you witness, don't pressure people—unless the Holy Spirit leads you to do it. Always keep yourself sensitive to the need for guidance. Always realize you are representing God. Use the Bible, but use it deftly, imaginatively. Don't let witness become rigamarole, a cut-and-dried formula. Invite the Holy Spirit to make you creative when you witness, pliable to divine guidance so you will be relevant to each individual need, because no two people are alike.

The Bible is the Sword of the Spirit, to be sure, but its main purpose is to serve as a healing implement of God's love, not as a rapier which you brandish in triumphant mastery over enemy warriors brought to contrition.

Evangelism is not bringing men to Christ but bringing Christ to men. It is not you succeeding in spiritual enterprise, but the Holy Spirit using you in the best utilization of those traits and talents by which you are endowed so you can fulfill the plan God has for you. Evangelism is God at work articulating His message through the human agency of His choice.

You!

10.

Maybe You *Should* Let George Do It

Winning men to Christ is a team experience, and the Holy Spirit is the team Captain!

Christians flourish at the game of passing the buck. They like to perform their oblations in comfort, and preferably in luxury. Any price paid for the faith should be properly discounted.

Nowhere do we cheat out worse than we do in the face of spiritual responsibility. We will serve on committees, spearhead fund drives, organize picnics, decorate banquets, contribute to lavish building programs, but we want George to do it when it comes to such front-line assignments as concerned prayer, searching and teaching the Scriptures, and especially, putting forth the sickle.

Well, frankly, there are functions of the Christian life which should be left to George. He may, for example, be an expert on building construction, a seasoned accountant, he might be musical.

The proverbial "George" possesses an abundance of talents. He belongs to the "they" family, included on the membership roster of every congregation. "They say" and "they won't approve" and "they run everything." But it also seems "they" are left the noble task of witness.

So then George, being a "they," can be counted upon to help us in our evangelism. The only hitch is that George many times can't function properly unless you and I have previously functioned properly.

As already indicated, witnessing often occurs as a cumulative effort. Some go so far as to insist no one comes to Christ without prior contact, especially in the case of young people caught fully in the modern mesh of atheistic materialism.

Now you and I dare not settle for halfhearted witness, then hide behind the premise of our having planted the seed for someone else to nurture and bring to harvest—which is why it becomes so important to be receptive and obedient to the promptings of the Holy Spirit.

You see, the Holy Spirit sometimes ordains for me to function as George!

I've told you the majority of my witness contacts fall in the preconversion category. It used to bother me. I couldn't bring myself to force someone to a decision, simply to add another scalp to my ecclesiastical belt, and yet I didn't want to be remiss in my responsibilities to God. We've considered the argument that no salesman is content to simply show a product and hope to later make a sale. A good salesman tries to close the deal on the spot.

The gaping hole in that argument is that you and I aren't the salesmen. The Holy Spirit is!

The more I ponder Scripture, the more I realize how much God does intend for me to be His instrument. I cannot command the Holy Spirit. I must permit the Holy Spirit to command me.

I have had times when I've gained excellent rapport with someone, when it seemed certain it would be my privilege to bring this person to a profession of faith, only to sense that I had carried the issue as far as I was meant to do.

For example, prior to the advent of jet travel, when a plane trip was an experience instead of just enough time to eat a meal, I sat beside a distinguished gentleman on a flight from Chattanooga to Chicago.

He was reading a secular magazine which featured an Easter article written by Jim Adair about a young Chicago hoodlum who professed faith before going to the electric chair. Jim, a close friend of mine, had asked me to go with him on one of his research visits to death row in Cook County Jail.

Quite obviously, I took this not as happenstance but as a signal from God to approach my seatmate. Wanting to be sure, however, I paused a few moments, praying for guidance.

Then he looked up.

"That's quite an article," I said, gesturing to the magazine. He nodded.

Nothing was said for a moment. I prayed for instructions, sensed no guidance to push the contact.

"It's refreshing to see one of our magazines printing religious material like this," he said.

"The article is particularly interesting to me," I told him.

"How is that?"

"The author's a personal friend. I was with him when he researched the article."

Now he gave me full attention.

"That must have been a sobering experience," he said.

"It was."

"I'd like to hear about it."

We talked all the way to Chicago. I learned he came from a Christian home but, unfortunately, had had parents who were long on the negatives of their faith and short on the positives. He was head of the music department at one of the Big Ten universities.

"I've pretty much gotten away from any kind of Bible orientation in my life," he told me.

But he asked questions, many of which I couldn't answer. I found he appreciated it when I told him I didn't have an answer, and listened all the more intently to what I said when I felt I did have an answer.

The more I talked to him, the more I could tell how hungry he was for spiritual genuineness. Yet I increasingly sensed his need for more time to think.

131

Years later, while on a filming assignment at his campus, I met him again. My pulse quickened, wondering if he might have closed the gap.

He gave no indication. But he did greet me warmly and say, "I've never forgotten our pleasant conversation on the plane. I still remember many of the things you said."

Please Lord, I implored silently, *is this the time for me to help this man make a decision?*

I could feel no positive guidance, and it bothered me. Was I being a coward, shunning responsibility?

Please, Lord!

He excused himself to go to an assignment.

I then met his assistant and, to my delight, found him to be a fine, evangelical Christian!

"We've been witnessing to him," the assistant said. "Frankly, you really started him thinking on that plane trip. He's often mentioned it to me."

"I nearly continued the witness now," I said, "but I felt constrained."

"That was the Lord's doing, Ken! He's so confused, caught between rebellion and the way he knows is right. All that's left is to make his decision, and he knows it. Pushing him now could be tragic."

Thanks, Lord! I breathed.

On another flight I sat revising a magazine article, a personality story about an outstanding Christian athlete I had interviewed.

The stewardess came by, took an interest in what I was doing, asked if she could have a look. Sitting on the arm of the seat across the aisle from me, she took each page as I revised it. I was preparing the final draft for my secretary to type when I got home, so it went rather quickly. I finished in about half an hour.

When I looked up, expecting her to hand the complete manuscript back to me, I was amazed to discover she had interested three or four passengers in the story and, page by page, my manuscript was making the rounds among them!

The stewardess asked many questions, as several of the passengers moved closer to listen. She wanted to know about my own philosophy of life, why I wrote these kind of articles, if I knew of additional athletes with this outlook.

Then we neared the airport, where I would deplane, and the stewardess excused herself to attend to flight duties. The passengers returned to their seats to obey the belt sign.

I will always remember the look in her eyes as we said good-bye at the door. That magazine article explained how the athlete went to the Bible for his answers in the search for faith. As I left the plane, I reminded God of His prescribed formula—one of His children planting the seed, another nurturing that seed, but God Himself reaping the harvest.

I flew with a young woman one afternoon who seemed very distraught, and I felt a compelling need to share my faith with her. The problem was that she appeared in no mood to talk with a strange man, however noble his intentions, so I gave up and began to occupy myself with some work I had brought along.

After a bit, we were served food. As we ate, the young woman began to talk—casually first, about nothing in particular. I prayed for guidance, feeling so sure I had a spiritual responsibility.

She said something about the sad state of affairs in the world today.

"That's why we need faith," I told her.

"Faith?" Her eyes blazed. "Faith in what?"

"In the assurance we can place ourselves in the care of one who will lead us through any kind of circumstance," I said.

"OK, where was this one you're talking about when my

husband and my two children burned to death in our apartment a month ago?"

Hardly anticipating this turn in the conversation, I was at a loss for words. I have learned this is good, for it makes me depend all the more upon the Holy Spirit for guidance. By His help, I carefully explained to this woman, who was still in obvious shock, how God does meet our needs in times of adversity. I told her of people I knew, people who had faced terrifying circumstances, and who had met every obstacle with the poise of faith.

From what she told me, it was obvious she and her husband had given little thought to eternal matters. Though I didn't press her for details, I got the impression the tragedy resulted from a fault of the husband's, perhaps drunkenness.

She settled back and closed her eyes. I wanted to tell her more, to invite her to accept my Savior into her life, but she gave me no opportunity. A sense of peace came to my heart, however. I had sown seed in this young woman's life. I prayed for the one who would reap the harvest.

Bob Bowman, one of the many young Missionary Aviation Fellowship pilots serving so uniquely in so many parts of the world, taught me an important lesson in this matter of prayer and evangelism.

"I can't find any place in the Bible," Bob said, "where God promises to answer our prayers for those who are lost."

His statement startled me.

"Do you know of any place?" he asked.

I raked my brain. I have a reasonable knowledge of the Bible. But the more I thought, and subsequently scoured a concordance, the more clearly I got the point.

We are told there is a spiritual harvest, a harvest ungathered for lack of harvesters, and we are urged to pray for harvesters more than for the harvest!

Praying for harvesters can surely involve praying for ourselves!

134

I try to make this strategic in my times of intercession. I am fortunate to have a number of friends, businessmen, who have a gift for the harvest. In those moments when I envy their gift, I ask God for forgiveness. I am grateful for the times, few though they may be, when I have had the privilege of bringing someone to the point of decision, for surely life has no greater joy than that of bringing someone to Christ!

Bringing men *to* Christ is, of course, wonderful, but as much joy should be ours in bringing men *toward* Christ.

Emerson Ward was of much help to me recently in the case of a personable young Hindu businessman. This fellow, born into India's highest caste, producer of a film of his own in India, was of invaluable aid to us in the production of *Journey to the Sky*, our film on the life of Sadhu Sundar Singh.

For example, he engineered the cooperation of an entire village, enabling us to procure scenes which would cost a fortune on a Hollywood back lot. The enthusiastic participation of the villagers amazed us.

One day, as we were working, he asked, "What do you think of my lovely Hindu friends?"

The question threw me off guard, and I said something about how much we appreciated the cooperation. It was the first time he had mentioned religion, which also caught me unprepared.

Later, after a well-turned production shot, he exclaimed, "I tell you, Mr. Anderson, here in my country Christianity is nothing!"

His words cut me like a knife.

"To me," I blurted awkwardly, "the Christian faith is everything!"

It was a poor beginning, but from this sprang a continuity of conversations which began to probe deeper and deeper into the subject, giving me repeated opportunities to witness. Mike Pritchard, former BBC television technician whom we had employed for the production, was with me. Mike's a fine person and a staunch Christian, and we both began to sense our friend was finding something different in our approach to him.

We learned, painfully, that this chap had been accused of gross dishonesty by a missionary, a charge later proved to be unfounded. Also, a lower-caste Christian (Sad to say, most Indian Christians come from the subordinate castes.) had recently accosted him with, "You'd better get converted or you'll die and go to hell."

Concern for this man began to weigh heavily upon my heart. I asked God for guidance, to keep my motives clean. Sure, it would make a great story to report how I had led a prominent Brahmin tea planter to Christ, but I wanted none of that. I wanted only to be my Lord's mouthpiece.

He spent nearly two months assisting us, but would take no payment for his service. In addition, his contacts and business acumen saved us hundreds of production dollars. So, as an expression of gratitude, we arranged to sponsor a trip for him to the United States on behalf of his tea business, since travel dollars are difficult to come by during these years of India's gallant struggle for fiscal stature on the world market.

Thus, as our guest, we had many additional opportunities for discussion. He arises early every morning, spends an hour in meditation and prayer, and asked me why this was not sufficient for salvation. He asked me how I knew for sure the Bible was God's Word, why I believed salvation could only be found in Christ.

Subsequently, he began talking about martyrdom. The man we had intended to use as the lead in our film, a recent Brahmin-caste convert to Christianity, had been put to death by his own brothers, who then bribed officials to falsify the death records.

At times my Hindu friend seemed so close. Yet I could

not bring myself to push him. The issues were too tense, the possible eventualities too grave.

His biggest barrier seemed to be the Bible's clear statement that *"all have sinned and fall short of the glory of God."* [1] This he could accept for a low-caste sweeper, a thief, but not for one of such altruistic aspirations as he.

One night, alone in my writing shack, I anguished in prayer. I knew I could not fail this man. Yet I couldn't even be sure how interested he was in the Christian faith. I've learned, by hard experience, that members of the Eastern world can show what seems to us to be spiritual interest but which, in reality, is little more than politeness.

It seemed more with this man, but how could I be sure?

Then that night, as I prayed, a strange phenomenon occurred. In an instant, the depressing burden on my heart lifted. I was still concerned for my friend, to be sure, but God seemed to say I had done all I could.

I had never had an experience quite like it before.

Next day I called Emerson Ward—a common occurrence around our area when someone has a witnessing problem. A businessman will bring a friend to the point of keen interest in salvation, then take him to Emerson for the final transaction.

Emerson is the epitome of spiritual tact and wisdom. He took to my Hindu friend like a brother. They made some trips together; Emerson invited him to his house. And, of course, the two spent a lot of time talking about the Christian faith.

I prayed much for Emerson!

Then one morning he came to my office. "I think we've done all we can for this fellow," Emerson said. "Every time I've wondered if I should perhaps press him to receive Christ, I've felt restrained. We'll just have to leave it in God's hands."

My Hindu friend returned to India. We corresponded, but with no inkling of revived spiritual interest. He began working closely with a missionary doctor on a business project for the doctor's hospital, and I prayed this might possibly lead to fruition.

One day I received a letter from the missionary, Dr. Geoffrey Lehman, whose hospital at the foot of the Himalayas compares with the work of the late Dr. Albert Schweitzer of Lambarene in my opinion.

He named my Hindu friend, adding, "We've had many opportunities to counsel with him, and he now admits to being a sinner."

My hopes are revived that he will one day come to the Savior!

And, much as I thrill at the adventure of actually leading someone to Christ, I'm still content to point men "toward" Christ preparatory to the time the Holy Spirit will use some "George" to complete the work.

The point is, don't try to run God's business. Succeeding in witness is not chalking up another convert. Succeeding in witness is speaking when God leads you to speak, and keeping your mouth shut when He leads you to keep silent. *"I planted, Apollos watered, but God was causing the growth."* 2

I was asked one weekend to participate in a Presbyterian laymen's retreat at a state park near my home. The pastor was one of those infectious doers, a human dynamo, a radiant evangel. He introduced me to one young couple at the retreat. The girl, a lovely creature, was pregnant.

"She's pregnant in more ways than one," he said as we walked on. "Both she and her husband are spiritually pregnant. It's a case of celestial obstetrics. Birth should come soon now."

Beautiful!

But please don't construe my viewpoint to mean that "letting George do it" is the hard-and-fast norm in witnessing. Somewhere down the line, someone has to be George!

My good friend Ernie Classen says, "There are two impor-

138

tant points in witness—tact and contact. The first is important, but not nearly as important as the second. People are never going to come to Christ unless Christians get through to them with the Lord's message."

What a wonderful experience, when you are the one who forges the final link in the chain!

A while ago I met a charming Jewish girl. She opened up to spiritual conversation like a blossom and, in a very short time, expressed her willingness to embrace her Messiah. I could have gone without food for a week, just thinking about my great privilege!

Speaking of Jewish folk, an actor we often use is, like my friend the advertising executive, named Russ Reed. Russ, the actor, is a converted Jew; Russ, the executive, a converted Gentile.

We had Russ out for a narration session one day, and he told me, "I frequently get calls from people who have Jewish neighbors and want me to come talk to them."

"What do you say?" I asked.

"I tell these people to talk to them themselves. In many ways, a Gentile can get farther witnessing to a Jew than I can."

Russ also told me of a unique experience he had just encountered. He works the "Unshackled" broadcast a lot, and as a result received a letter from a woman in one of the Southern states. She had recently been converted, and was concerned about an old boyfriend, Jewish, who had an office in the Loop. She wanted Russ to go see him.

"I checked the telephone book," Russ says, "and, sure enough, there was a lawyer by that name. I called to make an appointment. The receptionist insisted on knowing my purpose, but I would only tell her I had to see him. She finally agreed to the appointment, but puzzled me by saying, 'The conditions are that, if you don't take his advice, we will charge you five dollars.' "

At the hour of the appointment, Russ entered the man's office.

139

"OK," the lawyer blurted, "who's the problem—you or your wife?"

It turned out he was exclusively a divorce lawyer.

The man remembered the woman who had written to Russ, and listened courteously as Russ gave his witness.

"He thanked me," Russ says, "and just as I was leaving, he buzzed his secretary and told her not to charge me for the appointment."

It's a magnificent lineage, the facets which fit together in this procedure of composite witness. Don't shy away from your responsibility. You're timid, you fluster easily, you're not sure what to say.

You and many of the rest of us!

Get solidly into your mind the procedure God uses. He uses people, ordinary folks like you and me. He doesn't ask us to disgrace His cause by putting on a fanatical exhibition. He asks us to move in the stream of life, to be interested in people, thoughtful and considerate, always open to His guidance, always obedient to that guidance.

God will never ask you to do something for which He will not also supply the wisdom and strength to accomplish. Nowhere does this hold more true than in the adventure of telling others about His grace.

Think of witness as a chain, with you serving as one of the links. The contribution you make may be small but it can never be insignificant. As you rely upon the Holy Spirit for wisdom, you will be able to fulfill your responsibility.

"George" may have the special joy of harvest, but his big success depends on your not defaulting through a small failure.

11.
The High Cost of Silence

What happens when Christians renege on their responsibility to those outside the fold? The answer is clear and starkly tragic. But it needn't be!

I had heard pulpit accounts of indolent Christians who felt a strong compulsion to witness to someone, didn't, then the lost soul fell suddenly before the relentless scythe of the grim reaper.

I feared it might one day happen to me.

It did.

To a childhood friend in the Iowa farming community from which I spring.

He was an exemplary chap. One year, when we were both children, our family succeeded in getting him to our church's vacation Bible school. But his father was strongly antagonistic and permitted only this one brief exposure to the ecclesiastical world.

After coming into assurance of the Christian faith for myself, I developed a disturbing concern for my friend. I wanted to talk to him, often determined to on holidays home from college, but never did. I did take him to a youth conference once, occasionally slipped a tract into exchanges of correspondence, but that was it.

Then one day he was struck down in a freak farm accident.

I remember standing by his casket, my heart aching from the bite of its own questions. Why had I kept silent? Why had I not openly shared with this fine guy the reality of my faith? Why hadn't I invited him to Christ?

The week preceding his death, I sent him one of the fine

141

Good News tracts developed by Clyde Dennis, the man who did so much to lift hand-to-hand witness out of the doldrums of smudgy print and stories about the Civil War. It so poignantly spelled out the gospel message that I gave a duplicate to the father and mother as we stood together at the casket in the family living room.

Might there be the remote possibility of something remembered at the VBS, from one of the tracts, from that day at the youth conference?

I wish I knew for sure.

In those years, I saw witnessing from a different vantage than I do now, but let me clarify one point. I firmly believe it is my duty to not only be continually alert for guidance, but, whenever in situations of potential opportunity, to seek guidance.

Waiting for God to show one what to do, however, is no excuse for doing nothing.

By practicing the enriching technique of relating every event of life, every human encounter, everything to our dependence upon the Holy Spirit for guidance, rare indeed would be the case where no guidance is forthcoming. One either knows he should speak or knows he should keep silent.

"Follow Me," Jesus said, *"and I will make you fishers of men."* [1]

Following our Lord entails the deepest essence of what we've been discussing, our constant candidacy for the privilege of representing Him among those who need His grace.

What an awesome thought!

I would be reluctant to suggest the potential of human infallibility. Yet the Bible tells us that *"the steps of a good man are ordered by the Lord."* [2] We are human, yes, but let us be increasingly aware that the more we seek to please our God, the more we can depend upon the Holy Spirit for motivation.

I'm convinced no Christian will make a mess of his life

142

if each day he consciously places himself in God's control, acknowledging his need of Christ's lordship through the presence of the Holy Spirit in every action and decision of his day.

In honesty, however, I confess that, though I cherish the enrichment spiritual obedience brings to my life, I am many times disobedient. I do not deny willful disobedience, though more often it is simply that I succumb to the insidious wiles of Mr. Screwtape as he deftly plays his wits against my weaknesses.

Since boldness in the articulation of my faith is probably my greatest vulnerability, it is here where I'm sure I most often fail.

I and many of my brothers and sisters in the Christian way!

While working on a project in Japan, I had the opportunity of speaking before a group of high school students. One of them, a girl, seemed exceptionally alert and attentive. At the close of the session, she came directly to me.

"Last year I was an exchange student in the United States," she said.

"I hope you enjoyed our country," I told her.

"It was wonderful! I wish every young person in Japan could have the privilege I had. I wish young people from Communist China and eastern Europe could visit the United States and find what it is really like."

She sparkled with excitement as she told me of the kindnesses expressed to her She had been named homecoming queen. On her birthday, members of the school choir sang greetings over the school intercom.

"Was there anything about my country you didn't like?" I asked.

With typical Japanese politeness, she assured me there was nothing.

However, her eyes betrayed her, so I prodded a bit.

"No person is perfect," I said, "and with all the criticism America receives across the world these days, it's rather

143

obvious many people consider our nation far from perfect."

"That is one of the things I admire about your country," she said. "You are willing to take criticism."

She told me she was concerned about the people of America, about the way they took things for granted. She had, for example, looked forward to learning more about democracy, believing America to be the greatest democracy on earth, but had had a difficult time finding those who cared much about discussing the subject.

"Kids were more interested in dates and movies and television programs," she said. Her eyes brightened. "But they were very nice to me."

"Anything else?" I asked.

"You have beautiful schools," she continued, "much nicer and better equipped than schools in Japan. But so few kids seemed concerned about an education.

"In my country, we have a saying, 'Five fail, four pass.' It means if you sleep five hours a night, you will fail your graduation exams. If you only sleep four hours a night, you will pass your graduation exams. In Japan, I would study every night till I got too sleepy. Then I would go to bed, setting my alarm to ring again in four hours. But in America, kids only studied hard when exam time came. How can America remain a strong country if students are not more serious about their education?"

The texture of our conversation enabled me to introduce the Christian faith. A look of great sadness came to her face.

"Actually," she said, "I went to America for two reasons. I wanted to learn more about democracy, and I was interested in becoming a Christian."

"Did you become a Christian?" I asked.

She shook her head. "It would not be possible for me to ever become a Christian."

"Why?"

"I do not understand it."

144

How can Christianity be important
if Christians never talk about it...

"But Christianity is first of all something you experience."

"Let me explain."

I listened.

"Every Sunday in America," she continued, "I went to some church. The people I stayed with were very nice, but they seldom went to church. So I usually went alone. I loved the churches. You have such wonderful Christian songs. I liked the things the ministers said, too. Sometimes I would sit in church and pretend I was a Christian. I wanted to be one so much."

She turned away.

"I often lingered in the church after services. I thought perhaps someone would ask me if I wanted to become a Christian. No one ever did. I went to church many times, but no one talked to me about the Christian faith. How can Christianity be important if Christians never talk about it?"

I tried to salvage the situation, tried to explain how simply she could now relate her life to Christ, but it was too incomprehensible to her—the thought of having spent a year in a Christian country, a country which sent missionaries to Japan for the purpose of making converts, and yet finding no one concerned enough to help her.

Surely in the high school she attended, and most certainly in several of the churches, there were those who could have. Would they not have been directed to this girl, had they been asking God to guide them? Did God speak to someone, possibly to several, and they disobeyed?

We corresponded for several months, and in one letter she agreed to read suggested portions in the Bible. She wrote to tell me she found the Bible most interesting, and my hopes rose, but then one day I received a letter in which she said, "I have not written for some weeks now. I have been making an experiment. I decided not to read the Bible, but to read Buddhist scriptures instead, and I find I get along very well without the Bible."

She never corresponded with me again.

Disturbed, I wrote her story for *Campus Life* magazine, prayed someone in the western New York town where she spent the year in the United States would read the article.

One day I received a large, plain white envelope. It had no return address, but inside was a little monthly magazine published by the high school the girl had attended.

It reprinted my article in total.

At the top of the lead page were these words: "We all remember with much pleasure the one who is featured in this reprint. Many of us will be saddened by the way we failed to meet her need."

I can only hope I was led to this girl, as I feel sure I was, and that—even though she no longer writes—something of the concern I expressed will stay alive in her heart and, one day, bring her to a renewed search for the Christian faith.

Sometime later, I had a similar experience on board a Scandinavian Airlines jet flight from New York to Stockholm.

I had been exceptionally busy, clearing my desk for an extended motion-picture production assignment in the Orient, and as my wife drove me to the airport for the preliminary flight to New York, weariness nagged my mind and my body, and I asked God to make it possible for me to get a seat by myself on the SAS plane that night.

A warmth of assurance came to my mind, and I thanked God in advance.

I held a tourist ticket and, as you know, seats in the tourist section are arranged in threes. It's a sardine's experience if the flight is fully booked, but one sometimes has all three seats to himself and can push up the armrests and stretch out quite comfortably.

Arriving in New York, I transferred immediately to the Scandinavian Airlines lounge and presented my ticket to the girl at the counter. She processed it, gave me my seat assignment.

It was on the aisle. That meant someone else had the

window seat, giving me no prospect for the sleep I needed.

My spirits sagged. I felt chagrin toward God. I had prayed so definitely for a seat by myself so I wouldn't need to spend the long night sitting upright—invariably a head-throbbing experience for me—but my prayer went unanswered. How could I carry on business—God's business—in Stockholm the next day unless I got some rest?

The flight was called, and I boarded.

I took my seat on the aisle, opened my briefcase and selected some material I needed to brush up on for the next day's appointments. Several moments passed. Takeoff time neared. The two seats beside me remained vacant.

Perhaps I would have all three to myself after all!

But then, among last-minute passengers, someone came. I was aware of trousers slipping past me to the window seat, but I didn't look up.

The thistle of my innate hostility to strangers was in full flower!

The plane moved out onto the runway, subsequently took off. After four or five minutes I had the feeling of being looked at. I turned to the person beside me, discovered I was being intently scrutinized by a young Arab.

He grinned boyishly.

I returned the smile, my hostility waning. After all, it wasn't his fault the flight was as full as it was.

We struck up a conversation. He told me he had been in the U.S. for several months of training, prior to returning to his home in Jordan, where he would work as a pilot for Jordanian Airlines.

"You aren't going to my country by any chance?" he asked.

"No," I said. "I have some business in Stockholm tomorrow, and then I'll be flying on to India."

This fascinated him. He had long wanted to visit India, he said. He asked the purpose of my trip. I told him. Now I had his rapt attention.

"I tried out for a part in the film *Lawrence of Arabia,*"

he said, "but I guess I'm a better pilot than an actor. What're the names of some of your films? I went to quite a few movies when I was in America."

I told him we produced films for churches.

"They're about the Christian faith?" he asked.

I nodded.

Thereupon began one of the most engaging conversations I had ever had with someone from another country, as this chap probed me with questions about the Christian faith. They were superficial questions at first, and I replied to each carefully. I needed to be sure of his motives.

A stewardess brought dinner.

Pork.

Presuming my new acquaintance to be of the Muslim faith, and thus one who wouldn't touch pork, I was quite surprised to see him begin eating with considerable relish.

"Good thing I'm still on the way home," he said. "I like pork." He took a big bite. "Actually, I'm not much of a Muslim. I go to the mosque and all that, and I'll have to live without pork back home, but I don't think much of the Muslim religion. I think the Christian religion is better than Islam—much better."

Clearly, I knew God had just given me my cue to go on stage!

I began by complimenting many of the good traits I had observed among the people of Pakistan, the Persian Gulf and Iran, where I had worked.

"But you found a lot of fanatic Muslims, didn't you?" he asked. "Especially in Pakistan and the Persian Gulf? Whew! If I lived in either of those places, I'd go nuts. Jordan's bad enough, but it's pretty liberal in many ways, even though it is next door to Saudi Arabia."

"Ever been to Mecca?" I asked.

He shook his head. "I wouldn't waste the time."

"What is it that interests you so much about Christianity?"

"It's hard to say, because I don't know an awful lot about

150

it. I guess what's appealed to me most is how different the way of life is for people in a Christian country as compared to the way it is among us Arabs. It's as different as night and day, you might say. We're like night, you're like day."

By the time the stewardess removed our dinner trays, his questions had become so pointed I asked if he would like me to show him in the Bible what I had found as the basis for my faith. He was entirely agreeable.

Beginning, as I usually do in witnessing, with Romans 10:17, *"Faith comes by hearing, and hearing by the word of Christ,"* I took him briefly through the life of Jesus, to the cross and the empty tomb, to the Pauline requisites for experiencing the transformed life.

I felt a growing confidence he was ready to take the decisive step, right there beside me on the plane, and my heart sang with anticipation.

"You could receive Christ as your Savior right here and now," I said.

But then his countenance clouded.

"I need to think about this a little more," he said

"Why?" I asked, though not to pressure him.   .

"Well, it's a funny thing. Like I said, I've been real interested in Christianity, and I just might have become one under the right circumstances. But I do have my family to face, and my government expects all pilots to be faithful Muslims."

"What do you mean by right circumstances?"

He was pensive for a long moment.

"Well," he began, "it's this way. America overwhelmed me at first. It's a tremendous place. I knew Christianity must have had something to do with it. I wasn't sure what. But, anyway, many times when I prayed in the morning to Allah—I guess I'm really a maverick Muslim—anyway, when I'd pray to Allah, I asked to meet a Christian who was, well, who was really excited about his faith."

151

I cringed, remembered the girl from Japan, and asked, "You never found such a person?"

He shook his head, but a smile came to his face. "Not till now. Not till I met you."

On and on we talked. The lights were turned off on the plane. My weary bones cried for sleep, but I told God I'd gladly stay awake all night if I could help this fellow.

We came so close. It was plain to see how easily he might have been won during his stay in America. But now, heading home, about to meet his family, about to begin his job—

The best I could do was to supply him with a New Testament, which he promised to secretly study. He also gave me his Jordanian address so I could send him literature for further information.

The plane droned out into the darkness. I saw him grow weary. Release came to my heart, a sense of realization that I had done all I could do.

I pointed to the empty seat between us.

"Put down your armrest," I said. "That way you can stretch out a little more."

"You take the extra space," he said.

But I insisted. He was much shorter than I and I could see how much more practical it was for him to utilize the space, so he did.

I didn't mind. It didn't seem quite so distasteful now, sitting upright in a position which makes sleep just about impossible for me.

My friend soon slumbered. I stared out into the dimness, thanking God for intercepting my selfish desires with this magnificent opportunity.

Then one of the stewardesses came.

"Mr. Anderson," she whispered, "would you like a seat where you can stretch out and rest? There is an empty one at the back of the plane."

I had never had such a thing happen to me before, nor have I since. I'm sure I looked at her in utter disbelief. Then, grateful, I got up and followed her.

We came to the three empty seats, armrests out of the way. She had even put down a pillow and spread a blanket.

I thanked her profusely, then kicked off my shoes and stretched out for five hours of the most appreciated sleep I had had in a long time.

Lord, I prayed, *please forgive me! And thanks for the little detour You arranged before You answered my prayer!*

You may think it happenstance, the stewardess singling me out to have that place to rest. I had said nothing to her. There were many other passengers who would have to sit up uncomfortably through the night. Why did she choose me?

On the other hand, why should I question?

Do I believe God answers prayer or don't I? I asked for a good night's sleep, and now God was answering that prayer. I had also asked Him for guidance as to anyone to whom I might relate my faith. He answered that prayer too!

You see, we can trust the Holy Spirit to lead us. It really is valid to believe one represents God here on planet earth.

He uses us just as we are, limitations and all.

And, really, we have no limitations. For the Bible tells us we are *"fearfully and wonderfully made."* 3 We came into the world fully equipped to serve our God in the manner of His intention.

But, being human, we also possess the capacity to resist His intention, to thwart the Holy Spirit's guidance. *"Do not grieve the Holy Spirit,"*4 the Bible warns. We grieve Him when we disobey by refusing to follow the Holy Spirit's guidance.

What happens when we do this?

The experience of the girl from Japan is what happens. And the young man from Jordan. And the many, many other candidates for salvation elbowed out of their spiritual rights by lethargic Christians.

Not being a theologian, I prefer silence on such subjects as the sovereignty of God, predestination, man's freedom of choice. Bob Evans of Greater Europe Mission postulates that God crosses every man's path at least once in a redemptive encounter.

Possibly so.

What I am certain about is the clarity of our Lord's words when He said, *"You shall be witnesses unto Me."*

Of late, I've begun to suspect another ingredient.

The Bible warns, *"Where there is no vision, the people perish."* 5

I once took this to imply lack of vision, meaning lost men perish because they are unevangelized. Such a dark reality is surely indicated. But might it not probe even deeper? When we, by disobedience, deny ourselves vision—which, so far as I am concerned, simply means the Holy Spirit's guidance—squalor comes to our own souls. Time and talent we ought to have used to the glory of God "perish" univested, forever wasted instead of utilized for our Father's intended purpose.

But this need not be our lot.

If we begin where we are, whatever our traits and talents, whatever our circumstances—if we step by step move ourselves into the mainstream of the Holy Spirit's guidance, and if we are obedient to that guidance, we will discover the principle, *"I planted, Apollos watered, but God was causing the growth"* not only involves the winning of lost men but the coming of abundance into our own lives as well!

Here, then, is the sum of it.

I'm the same person I've always been. As long as I live, I'll be prone to cowardice.

But being the same person does not mean I must continue to grovel in the same weakness. I am what I am—plus God!

That's the song of it.

A coward, a failure-prone human being, in the process of the continual discovery of my Lord's sufficiency—the Lord who lives in me through the Holy Spirit—and, consequently, my ever widening horizons of potential.

Yet I must exercise one all-important caution.

Resting on God's promises does not mean relaxing upon my privileges. Just as one can become unfortunately fixated on a given point of doctrine, to the exclusion of related truths in Scripture which bring that doctrine into its fullest perspective, so I dare not settle for a spiritual mentality which—professing to be scriptural—becomes nothing more than a religious innoculation against concern and fervor.

Prerequisite to knowing you are in the will of God is to have a continuous concern for those who are lost.

In sketching the final chapter of this book, wondering how my Lord would have me conclude it, I faced a blank wall. In my learning process as a Christian, I have discovered there are really no blank walls at all, no dead-end streets.

Plainly, God was telling me to wait—always good advice for a writer who finds that placing a manuscript on the shelf for a time makes for smoother copy in the subsequent revision process.

While awaiting guidance, my schedule involved a flight to Japan to set up a student-evangelism film project we were about to do. The plane, a 747 jumbo jet, was only sparsely loaded so I had a seat to myself.

A Japanese businessman sat across the aisle, one seat ahead, and as I got out my briefcase and began mulling once again over a possible concluding paragraph for this chapter, I wondered if perhaps I ought to speak with this man, if in our conversation might appear something appropriate to this instance.

How awesome are the ways of our wonderful Lord!

While I hesitated, a GI came and sat beside the man. The GI had a large Bible in his hands.

"Pardon me, sir," the soldier said. "Do you speak English?"

"Yes, I do," the man replied, obviously eager for cordial conversation.

"Then I want to tell you that Jesus loves you!"

My ears came to full alert and for several moments I

listened as the GI witnessed to the man. I could find points to criticize in his procedure, but there was no questioning the sincerity of his motive, the love in his heart.

The Japanese politely but pointedly resisted the message. So the soldier went to numerous others in our cabin, until someone complained and the steward ordered him to his seat.

Looking back, I saw how concerned he was, how disappointed, and so I went and talked to him. He was joyous at meeting another Christian.

"These people are lost," he said. "We've got to tell them about Jesus."

I shared with him my experiences in seeking the guidance of the Holy Spirit.

"But if you know people are lost," he countered, "and if you've got the time to do it, isn't the opportunity guidance?"

I learned he was stationed in Vietnam. Even though President Nixon was then endeavoring to wind down the war, this soldier was out in the field every day facing the enemy.

"I've seen a lot of my buddies blown up right beside me," he said. "I wouldn't judge anybody, but as near as I know, those guys went to hell."

Back at the airport in San Francisco, he told me, an officer had allowed him two minutes to speak to a planeload of replacements just ready to leave for Indo-China. His eyes sparkled as he related how intently they listened to his witness of what it meant to have Christ with him in times of supreme danger.

I'm sure God put that young man on the plane, not only for those who needed salvation but as a witness to me, a warning never to become matter-of-fact in facing up to my responsibility in witness.

Because, you see, when I looked at the name tag above his battle ribbons, I saw that his name, like mine, was *Anderson!*

156

NOTES

Chapter 1

1. Ro. 10:17.
2. 1 Co. 3:6, NASB.
3. Ps. 126:6.
4. Ro. 1:16, NASB.

Chapter 2

1. 2 Co. 12:9, NASB.
2. 2 Co. 2:14, NASB.

Chapter 3

1. Eze. 3:18-19, NASB.

Chapter 4

1. Ac. 1:6, NASB.
2. Ac. 1:7-8, NASB.

Chapter 5

1. Jn. 15:5, NASB.
2. Eph. 2:10, NASB.
3. Jn. 17:16-18, NASB.
4. Ps. 100:3, NASB.
5. Heb. 11:13, NASB.
6. Ps. 37:4, NASB.
7. Is. 30:15.
8. Gal. 5:22, NASB.

Chapter 6

1. Col. 2:6, NASB.
2. Pr. 23:7.
3. Phil. 2:5.
4. 2 Co. 5:17, NASB.
5. 2 Co. 12:9*a*.
6. 2 Co. 12:9*b*-10.
7. Phil. 2:12-13.
8. Ro. 8:28, NASB.
9. Mk. 8:36, NASB.
10. 2 Pe. 3:18, NASB.
11. Jn. 10:10.
12. Phil. 2:12.

Chapter 7

1. Pr. 11:30, NASB.

Chapter 8

1. Col. 1:27.
2. Phil. 2:13, NASB.
3. Ps. 32:8.
4. Job 35:10.
5. Lk. 2:52, NASB.
6. Ro. 12:2.
7. 1 Th. 5:17.
8. 2 Co. 3:2.
9. 1 Jn. 5:14, NASB.

Chapter 9

1. Ja. 4:8.
2. 1 Th. 5:21, NASB.
3. Ro. 1:17, NASB.
4. Ja. 1:5.
5. Ro. 10:17, NASB.
6. 1 Co. 3:6, NASB.

Chapter 10

1. Ro. 3:23, NASB.
2. 1 Co. 3:6, NASB.

Chapter 11

1. Mt. 4:19, NASB.
2. Ps. 37:23.
3. Ps. 139:14.
4. Eph. 4:30, NASB.
5. Pr. 29:18.